How

How to Knit

Your Step By Step Guide to Basic Knitting Plus Two Patterns

HowExpert with Deborah C. Harding

Copyright HowExpert™
www.HowExpert.com

For more tips related to this topic, visit HowExpert.com/knit.

Recommended Resources

- HowExpert.com – Quick 'How To' Guides on All Topics from A to Z by Everyday Experts.
- HowExpert.com/free – Free HowExpert Email Newsletter.
- HowExpert.com/books – HowExpert Books
- HowExpert.com/courses – HowExpert Courses
- HowExpert.com/clothing – HowExpert Clothing
- HowExpert.com/membership – HowExpert Membership Site
- HowExpert.com/affiliates – HowExpert Affiliate Program
- HowExpert.com/writers – Write About Your #1 Passion/Knowledge/Expertise & Become a HowExpert Author.
- HowExpert.com/resources – Additional HowExpert Recommended Resources
- YouTube.com/HowExpert – Subscribe to HowExpert YouTube.
- Instagram.com/HowExpert – Follow HowExpert on Instagram.
- Facebook.com/HowExpert – Follow HowExpert on Facebook.

Publisher's Foreword

Dear HowExpert Reader,

HowExpert publishes quick 'how to' guides on all topics from A to Z by everyday experts.

At HowExpert, our mission is to discover, empower, and maximize talents of everyday people to ultimately make a positive impact in the world for all topics from A to Z...one everyday expert at a time!

All of our HowExpert guides are written by everyday people just like you and me who have a passion, knowledge, and expertise for a specific topic.

We take great pride in selecting everyday experts who have a passion, great writing skills, and knowledge about a topic that they love to be able to teach you about the topic you are also passionate about and eager to learn about.

We hope you get a lot of value from our HowExpert guides and it can make a positive impact in your life in some kind of way. All of our readers including you altogether help us continue living our mission of making a positive impact in the world for all spheres of influences from A to Z.

If you enjoyed one of our HowExpert guides, then please take a moment to send us your feedback from wherever you got this book.

Thank you and we wish you all the best in all aspects of life.

Sincerely,

BJ Min
Founder & Publisher of HowExpert
HowExpert.com

PS...If you are also interested in becoming a HowExpert author, then please visit our website at HowExpert.com/writers. Thank you & again, all the best!

COPYRIGHT, LEGAL NOTICE AND DISCLAIMER:

COPYRIGHT © BY HOWEXPERT™ (OWNED BY HOT METHODS). ALL RIGHTS RESERVED WORLDWIDE. NO PART OF THIS PUBLICATION MAY BE REPRODUCED IN ANY FORM OR BY ANY MEANS, INCLUDING SCANNING, PHOTOCOPYING, OR OTHERWISE WITHOUT PRIOR WRITTEN PERMISSION OF THE COPYRIGHT HOLDER.

DISCLAIMER AND TERMS OF USE: PLEASE NOTE THAT MUCH OF THIS PUBLICATION IS BASED ON PERSONAL EXPERIENCE AND ANECDOTAL EVIDENCE. ALTHOUGH THE AUTHOR AND PUBLISHER HAVE MADE EVERY REASONABLE ATTEMPT TO ACHIEVE COMPLETE ACCURACY OF THE CONTENT IN THIS GUIDE, THEY ASSUME NO RESPONSIBILITY FOR ERRORS OR OMISSIONS. ALSO, YOU SHOULD USE THIS INFORMATION AS YOU SEE FIT, AND AT YOUR OWN RISK. YOUR PARTICULAR SITUATION MAY NOT BE EXACTLY SUITED TO THE EXAMPLES ILLUSTRATED HERE; IN FACT, IT'S LIKELY THAT THEY WON'T BE THE SAME, AND YOU SHOULD ADJUST YOUR USE OF THE INFORMATION AND RECOMMENDATIONS ACCORDINGLY.

THE AUTHOR AND PUBLISHER DO NOT WARRANT THE PERFORMANCE, EFFECTIVENESS OR APPLICABILITY OF ANY SITES LISTED OR LINKED TO IN THIS BOOK. ALL LINKS ARE FOR INFORMATION PURPOSES ONLY AND ARE NOT WARRANTED FOR CONTENT, ACCURACY OR ANY OTHER IMPLIED OR EXPLICIT PURPOSE.

ANY TRADEMARKS, SERVICE MARKS, PRODUCT NAMES OR NAMED FEATURES ARE ASSUMED TO BE THE PROPERTY OF THEIR RESPECTIVE OWNERS, AND ARE USED ONLY FOR REFERENCE. THERE IS NO IMPLIED ENDORSEMENT IF WE USE ONE OF THESE TERMS.

NO PART OF THIS BOOK MAY BE REPRODUCED, STORED IN A RETRIEVAL SYSTEM, OR TRANSMITTED BY ANY OTHER MEANS: ELECTRONIC, MECHANICAL, PHOTOCOPYING, RECORDING, OR OTHERWISE, WITHOUT THE PRIOR WRITTEN PERMISSION OF THE AUTHOR.

ANY VIOLATION BY STEALING THIS BOOK OR DOWNLOADING OR SHARING IT ILLEGALLY WILL BE PROSECUTED BY LAWYERS TO THE FULLEST EXTENT. THIS PUBLICATION IS PROTECTED UNDER THE US COPYRIGHT ACT OF 1976 AND ALL OTHER APPLICABLE INTERNATIONAL, FEDERAL, STATE AND LOCAL LAWS AND ALL RIGHTS ARE RESERVED, INCLUDING RESALE RIGHTS: YOU ARE NOT ALLOWED TO GIVE OR SELL THIS GUIDE TO ANYONE ELSE.

THIS PUBLICATION IS DESIGNED TO PROVIDE ACCURATE AND AUTHORITATIVE INFORMATION WITH REGARD TO THE SUBJECT MATTER COVERED. IT IS SOLD WITH THE UNDERSTANDING THAT THE AUTHORS AND PUBLISHERS ARE NOT ENGAGED IN RENDERING LEGAL, FINANCIAL, OR OTHER PROFESSIONAL ADVICE. LAWS AND PRACTICES OFTEN VARY FROM STATE TO STATE AND IF LEGAL OR OTHER EXPERT ASSISTANCE IS REQUIRED, THE SERVICES OF A PROFESSIONAL SHOULD BE SOUGHT. THE AUTHORS AND PUBLISHER SPECIFICALLY DISCLAIM ANY LIABILITY THAT IS INCURRED FROM THE USE OR APPLICATION OF THE CONTENTS OF THIS BOOK.

COPYRIGHT BY HOWEXPERT™ (OWNED BY HOT METHODS)
ALL RIGHTS RESERVED WORLDWIDE.

Table of Contents

Recommended Resources 2

Publisher's Foreword.. 3

Introduction 7

Chapter 1: Needles 10

Chapter 2: Yarn 13

Chapter 3: Gauge 16

Chapter 4: Necessary Tools 18

Chapter 5: Patterns and Abbreviations 23

Chapter 6: How to Cast On 27

Chapter 7: The Knit Stitch... 35

Chapter 8: The Purl Stitch... 43

Chapter 9: How to Increase Stitches 49

Chapter 10: How to Decrease Stitches 56

Chapter 11: How to Join Yarn.................................... 65

Chapter 12: Binding Off... 68

Chapter 13: How to Finish A Project 75

Chapter 14: Blocking 83

Chapter 15: Care 92

Chapter 16: Stitch Patterns....................................... 97

Chapter 17: How to Join Seams............................. 108

Chapter 18: Scarf Pattern 121

Chapter 19: Arm Warmer Pattern 130

Chapter 20: Tips and Tricks.....................................133

Chapter 21: Conclusion..155

About the Expert 160

Recommended Resources 161

Introduction

Knitting is a comforting past time that produces concrete results. Make a scarf, a blanket, mittens or other wearable fashions using yarn and two or more knitting needles. Knitting is a hobby that is portable. Take it on a trip, take it to work to do at lunch, or relax on the front porch or in front of the TV and knit. Anyone can learn how to knit and the action will bring calmness to the mind and body.

In order to knit, learn only two major types of stitches. Once those two stitches are learned, the knitter can create just about anything. Those two stitches are the knit stitch and the purl stitch. Different combinations, adding or decreasing stitches and altering the stitch slightly make it possible to create sweaters, gloves, socks and other things in all different patterns, shapes and colors.

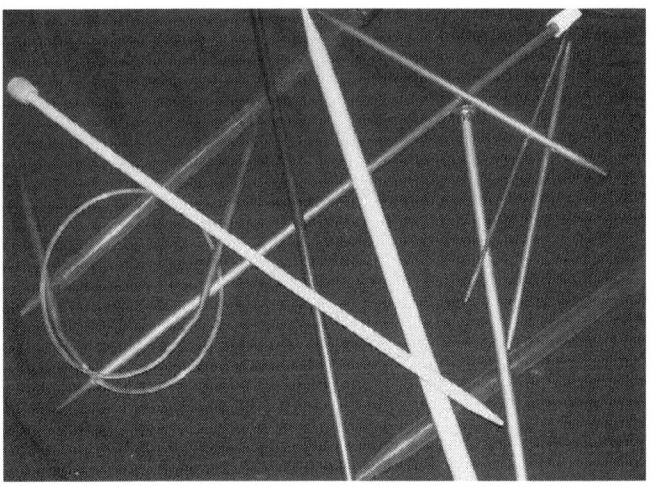

Illustration 1: Types of Knitting Needles

History

Records as far back as AD 200 report that weaving wool using two or more needles made cloth used for clothing, blankets and other objects within the community. Knitted cloth, instead of weaving thread on a loom, makes the fabric stretch better and it snaps back into shape quicker. The ancients used the knitting technique to make clothing that needed to stretch, but stay close to the body without sagging. Included were stockings, leggings, gloves and other garments. The oldest known knitted artifact is, in fact, a sock. Middle Eastern and Egyptian tombs showed evidence of knitted items from ancient days.

The Spanish employed Muslim knitters to make gloves, covers for cushions, and wearable garments from yarn. In Scotland during the 17th century and continuing into the 18th, being a knitter was an actual occupation. Heavy knitted sweaters protected Scottish fishermen during the winter as the wool had a waterproof effect. The Scots created some of the most intricate knitted patterns like the cable stitch and Aran stitch.

During the industrial revolution, spinning wool and knitting procedures mechanized and became less expensive. Soon people depended more on mass produced knitwear than taking up needles and knitting themselves. A resurgence of the craft took place in the early 21st century with the development of interesting yarns using llama hair, cotton, silk and bamboo. Today, there are thousands of knit patterns available to the public for baby clothes, gloves, hats, sweaters, afghans, toys and just about anything else.

This guide will focus on the different stitches, patterns and how to make a sampler and a few other projects.

Chapter 1: Needles

Knitting needles come in a variety of sizes and lengths. Metal needles are the best for a beginner, but needles come in wood and plastic too. The most important feature of the needle is to be as smooth as possible, so the yarn easily slips on and off.

TYPES

Straight Needles are the classic type of knitting needle and have a straight shaft with a pointy end and a disk or ball at the other to keep the stitches on the needle. Metal and plastic needles have a disk or cork-like end with the needle size imprinted at the top. Bamboo needles often have a ball at the top with the size is burned into the needle itself near the top.

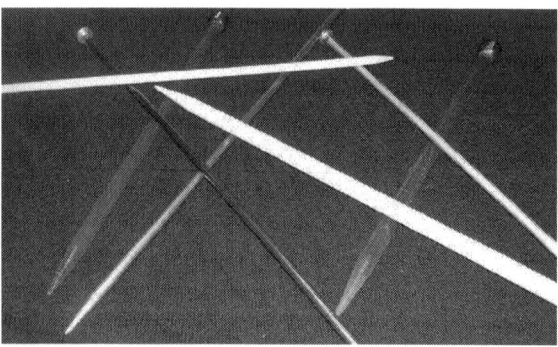

Illustration 2: Plastic, Bamboo and Aluminum Straight Needles

Double Pointed Needles have points at both ends and usually combine in three's or four's to make socks, gloves, hats or anything that knits around in a circle. The have points at both ends so that the stitches can slip on and off both ends.

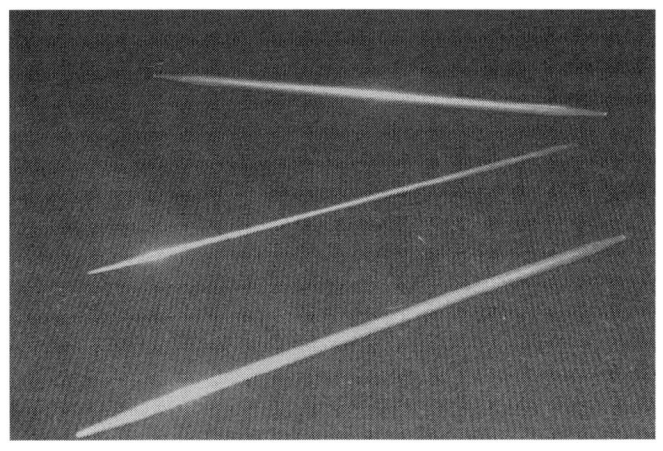

Illustration 3: Double Pointed Needles

<u>Circular Needles</u> are two needles joined together by a thin, flexible cable on which the stitches fit. Circular needles are good to use when make a piece with just one seam knitted in the round, or a piece that has too many stitches to fit on standard, straight needles.

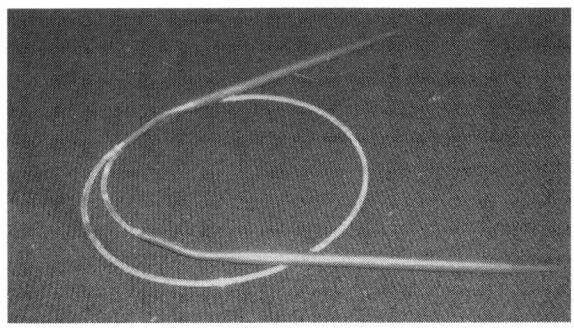

Illustration 4: Circular Needles

It is best for beginners to start out using straight needles as they are much easier to work with.

SIZE

The diameter of the needles indicates its size. US sizes run from 0 to 50 with size 6 to 10 being the most popular sizes. European and Canadian needles use metric numbers to label them. Both types come in a variety of lengths. The pattern used dictates the size and sometimes the length of the needles used.

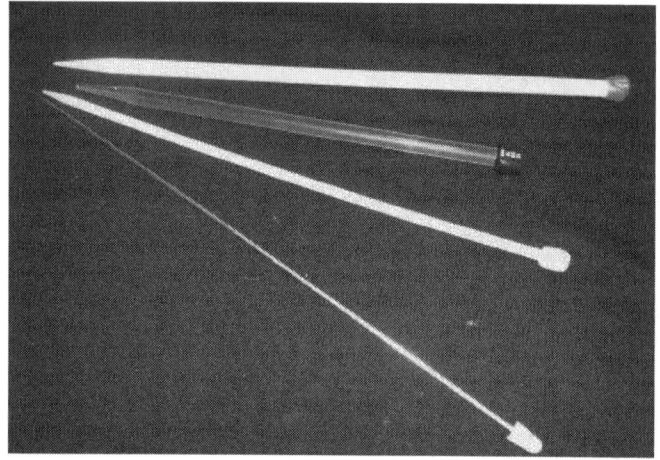

Illustration 5: Variety of Straight Needles

The European equivalent to a US size 7 needle is 4.5 mm and the equivalent to a US size 10 needle is 6.00 mm.

Chapter 2: Yarn

The multitude of available yarn is astounding. Yarn comes in all textures, colors and thicknesses. Choose the proper yarn for the project at hand. Patterns will specify the correct type of yarn to use.

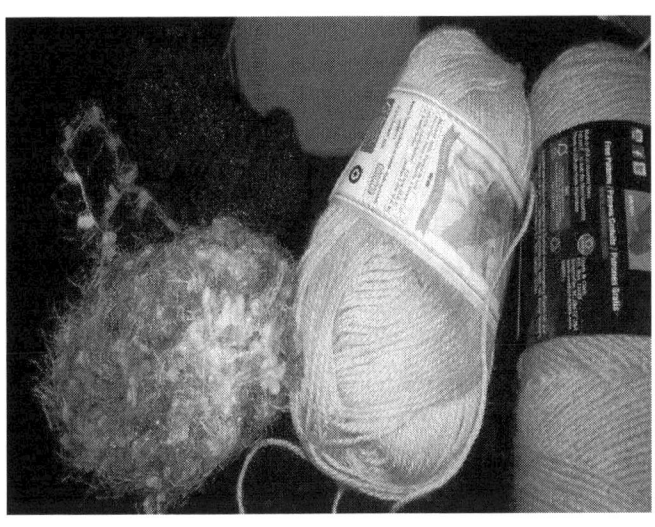

Illustration 6: Worsted, Baby, Sock and Novelty Yarn

Sheep wool, silk, cotton, linen, animal hair, acrylic fibers, nylon, rayon and other substances all are used to make yarn. When just learning how to knit, use acrylic yarn as it is easier to handle and less expensive than other types.

All yarn has a ply. This is the amount of strands twisted together to make one strand of yarn. Yarn that is 4-ply has four strands, and is the easiest to use for the beginning knitter.

Yarn comes in skeins, balls and hanks. A skein is one portion of yarn wound into an oblong shape and held together with a paper label around the middle. Some handmade yarns do not have the label, but should have some indication of what the yarn is made from, how to care for it and how many plies were used to make the yarn. If the yarn does not come with this information, it is best to steer clear of it.

Handmade yarn is usually twisted and formed into a circle. The yarn from the hank is best wound into a ball first in order to keep it from tangling.

Some yarn comes in balls where the yarn comes off the outside, or it is wound so that it is pulled from the inside of the ball. Anyone can wind a skein or hank of yarn into a ball simply by tearing off a little rectangle of paper and folding it in half. Place the end of the yarn so it is sticking out of one end just a few inches. of yarn instead, but most likely the yarn will come in a skein and start winding the yarn around the paper. Once an oval is made wind sideways and longways around the paper making sure the end still sticks out. When finished winding all the yarn pull the paper out leaving the end sticking out. Use this end to start the project.

The label on the yarn imparts the ply, type of yarn and other information needed like care of garment. The ply indicator will look like a skein of yarn inside a little white square. On the label of the yarn will be a number.

Illustration 7: Label for 4-Ply Yarn

Common yarn weights vary from 0 to 6 with 0 being very thin used for lacework and 6 being heavy for super bulky projects. Medium size, also called size 4, is best for beginning projects while yarns marked with 2 make good socks because it is thin enough to be comfortable within a shoe. Yarn marked with 5 works well for winter blankets or mittens because it is very dense. Always knit thin yarn with thin needles and bulky yarn with large needles.

Chapter 3: Gauge

Gauge is very important in knitting. If the gauge is not right, the project tends to be too big or too small.

Gauge is the number of stitches needed to knit 1 inch in length, and the number of rows needed to make 1 inch. Some knitters work their stitches loosely while others pull it tight making the gauge slightly bigger or smaller than it should be. Using a thicker or thinner yarn that what is called for in the pattern can affect gauge.

To check the gauge, make a small square with 20 stitches. Knit until the square measures 3 inches. Place the finished square on a table and flatten it out. See how many stitches made 1 inch and how many rows made 1 inch. It should match the gauge specified in the pattern.

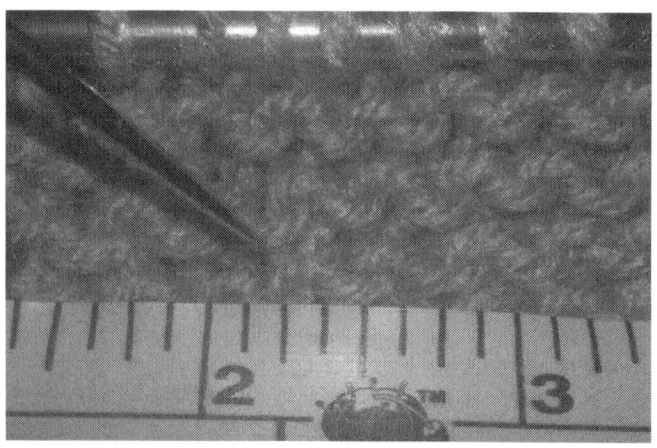

Illustration 8: Measure stitches horizontally

The gauge for the above square is 5 stitches = 1 inch. The gauge for the square below measures 8 rows = 1 inch.

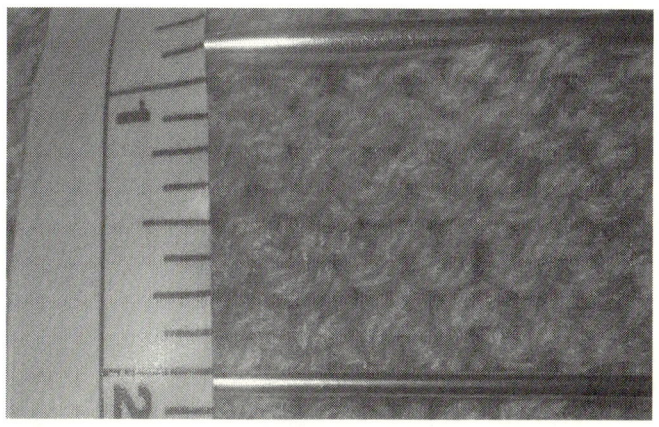

Illustration 9: Measure stitches vertically

Chapter 4: Necessary Tools

Knitting requires some other equipment besides yarn and needles. This equipment includes:

1. A ruler or measuring tape measures gauge and length of the project. Many patterns require measurements to know how long or wide to make pieces of the garment.

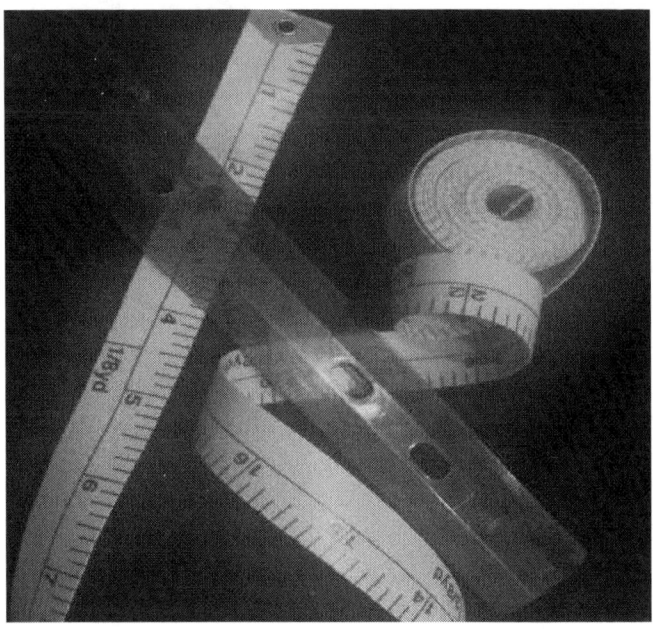

Illustration 10: Ruler and Tape Measure

2. Scissors cut the yarn when changing color or finishing the piece. Always use scissors instead of tearing the yarn apart. Tearing can cause the yarn to separate and one ply might be pulled harder than the other three causing a pucker.

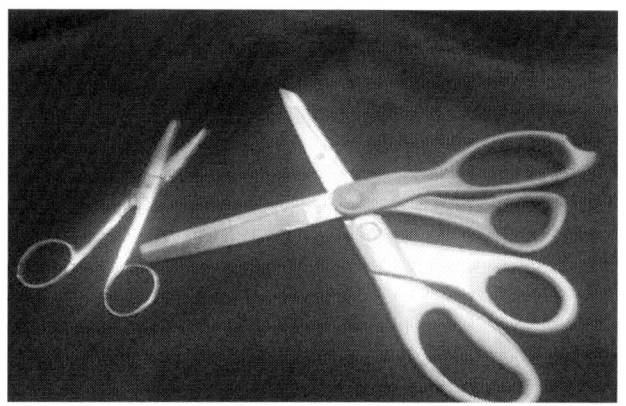

Illustration 11: Scissors

3. Blunt yarn needles come in plastic or metal and have very large eyes that allow the yarn to fit through. Yarn needles are not sharp because it is easy to work them through knitted yarn without having a sharp point. Knitted cloth has lots of little holes where the needle can easily penetrate. Yarn needles stitch components of a pattern together. An example would be stitching a sleeve to the body of a sweater.

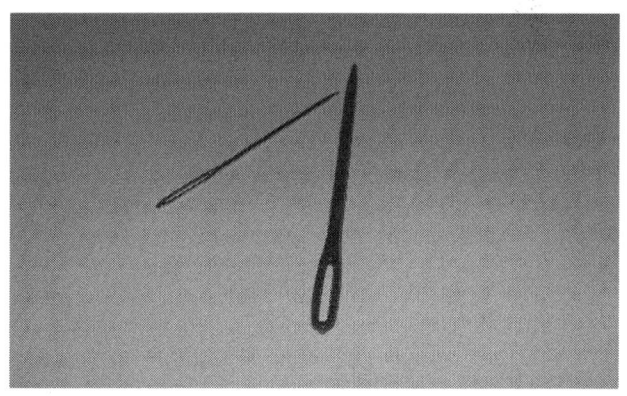

Illustration 12: Blunt Large Eye Yarn Needle

4. Stitch Markers are plastic rings that come in a variety of sizes and colors. They curl around and are sometimes open so that they are easily slipped over a stitch or over the needle to mark certain parts of the pattern.

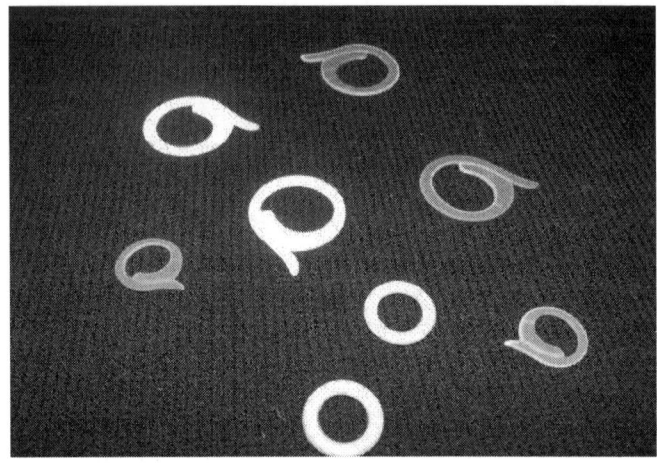

Illustration 13: Stitch Markers

5. Stitch Holders look like big safety pins. They hold stitches temporarily in order to get them out of the way of other stitches that receive more rows. An example of this would include making a mitten. The finger part of the mitten is put on a stitch holder while the thumb is worked. Once the thumb is done, the finger part of the mitten is put back on the needles and knitting can continue.

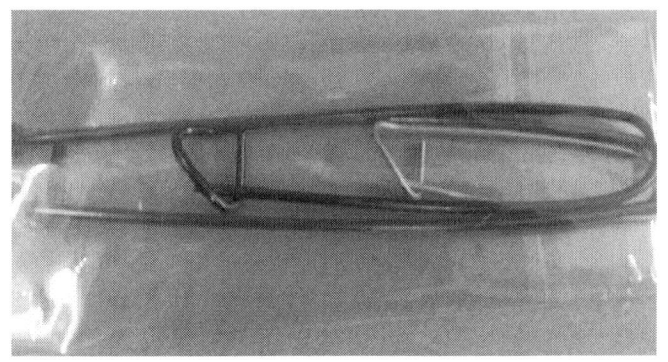

Illustration 14: Stitch Holders

Stitch Holders

6. Stitch Counters sometimes slip over the to the stopper end of one knitting needle. They have little wheels with numbers on them that indicate the number of rows. After each row is stitched, the knitter changes the number one up. The numbers usually go from 0 to 99.

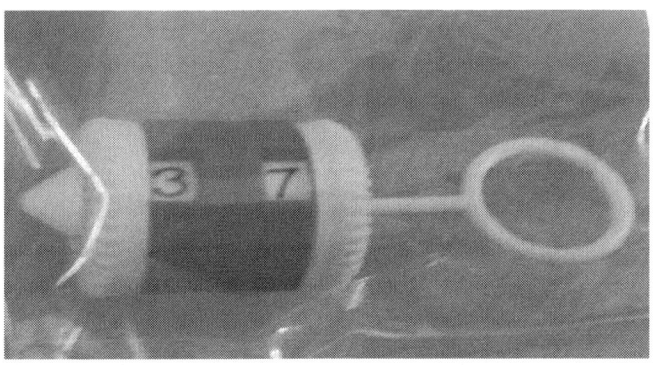

Illustration 15: Stitch Counter

A beginning knitter does not need all these tools at first. They need the yarn, needles, a measuring tool and scissors. The other tools can wait until the knitter decides that they wish to do more knitting and go on to more complicated patterns.

Chapter 5: Patterns and Abbreviations

Always choose patterns that include the following:

- Materials needed including type of yarn and needle size
- Gauge for stitches per length and per row
- Has easy to read directions
- Has a photo of the finished project to compare

Most patterns come in one size, but they give alternates for other sizes. These show up in parenthesis within the pattern. Here is an example: Knit 4 (5, 6, 6). The number 4 is for small, 5 is for medium, the first 6 is for large and the last 6 is for extra-large.

Reading a knitting pattern is like reading a map or a different language. Abbreviations are used and each abbreviation means the same thing in all patterns. The abbreviations are generally universal, but most patterns print the abbreviation key at the end of the pattern. If it is not there, find most standard abbreviations online or in other books about knitting. Many times, a special combination of stitches is used over and over again to make a specific pattern within the pattern. These stitches may be given special names that are unique to each pattern and they are presented at the beginning of the pattern.

The following are a few of the most common knitting abbreviations and their meaning:

Approx = Approximately

beg = beginning

bet = between

BO = bind off

CC = contrasting color

cm(s) = centimeter(s)

CO = cast on

dec = decrease

dpn(s) = double pointed needle(s)

g st = garter stitch

in(s) = inches

inc = increase

k = knit

k2tog = knit two together

kf&b = knit in front and back of stitch (in order to increase stitches)

kwise = knit wise (sometimes a pattern will want you to slip a stitch off the carrier needle to the   receiving needle without doing anything more to it. The point of the needle is inserted as if to knit, as opposed to purl, and slid off onto the receiving needle.

LH = left hand

LT = left twist

MC = main color

meas = measures

mm(s) = millimeter(s)

ndl(s) = needle(s)

oz = ounce

p = purl

p2tog = purl 2 together

pM = place marker

psso = pass slipped stitch over knit (or purl) stitch

pwise = purlwise (see knitwise)

rem = remaining

rep(s) = repeats

RH = right hand

rnd = round

RT = right twist

sk = skip

skp = slip, knit pass stitch over (a method of decreasing)

sl = slip

sl st = slip stitch

sl1k = slip one, knitwise

sl1p = slip one, purlwise

st st = stockinette stitch

st(s) = stitch(es)

tbl = through back loop

tog = together

Chapter 6: How to Cast On

Casting on is the first step in beginning to knit. The yarn has to go on the needles to start. This is the beginning instruction on how to make a sampler of stitches used to practice. Choose size 8 or 10 needles in metal or plastic and an inexpensive 4-ply, medium weight acrylic yarn. This sampler requires 20 stitches to be cast on.

Before casting on measure a tail of yarn, coming from the skein, that is 1 inch per stitch plus 6 extra inches. The sampler has 20 stitches, which equals 20 inches. Add 6 more inches for a total of 26 inches.

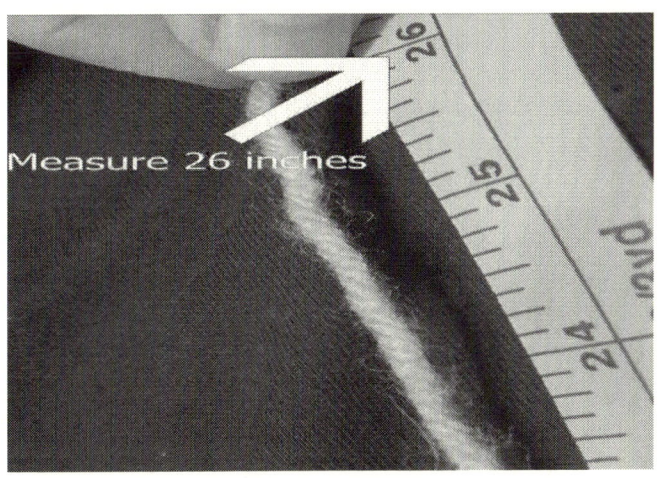

Illustration 16: Measuring Tail for Casting On

The following is directions for how to cast on:

1. Make a slip knot leaving the 26-inch tail a whole 26 inches.

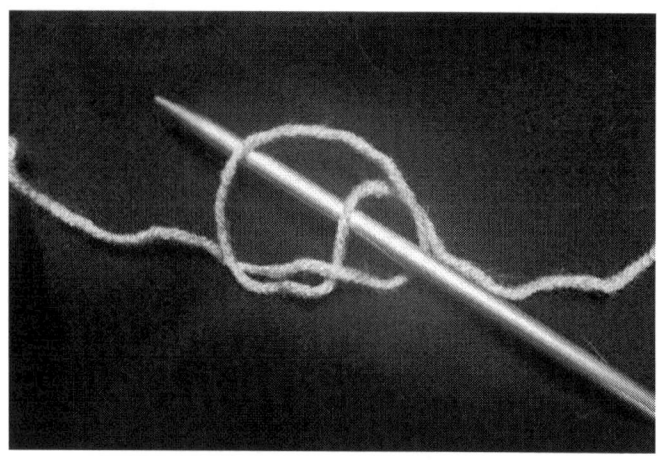

Illustration 17: Slip Knot

2. Insert one needle into the knot and pull tight. Insert needle into slip knot.

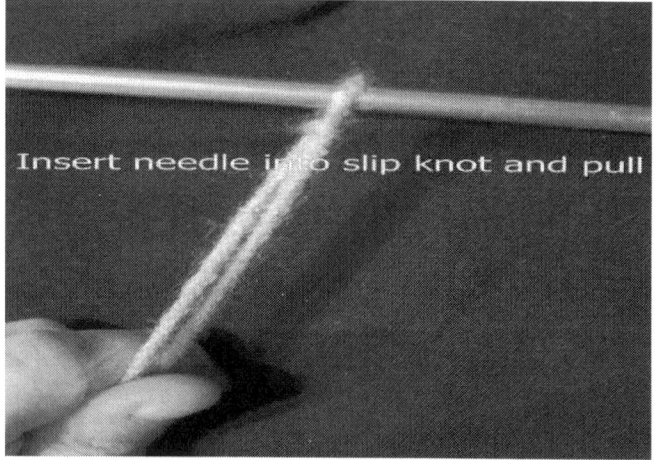

Illustration 18: Pull Tight to Secure Knot

3. Bring the 26-inch tail to the right toward the stopper end of the needle and hold the tail

attached to the skein, called the skein tail, with the left hand toward the point of the needle.

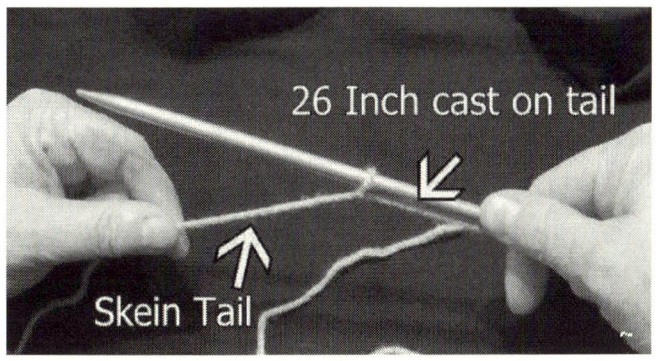

Illustration 19: Hold Tails

4. Also hold the top of the needle in the left hand and with the right hand, stabilize it down further toward the stopper.

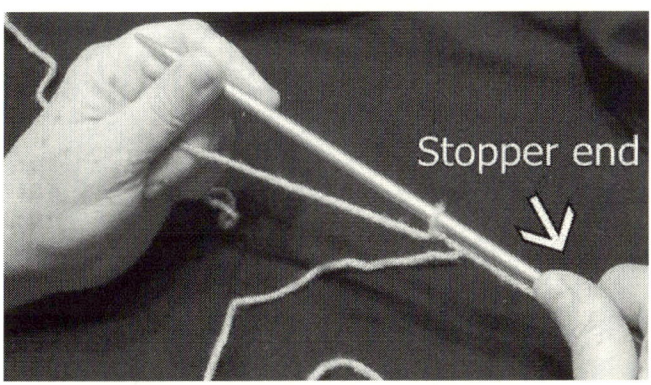

Illustration 20: Stabilize Needle

5. Take the left-hand thumb and bring it under the yarn to make a loop.

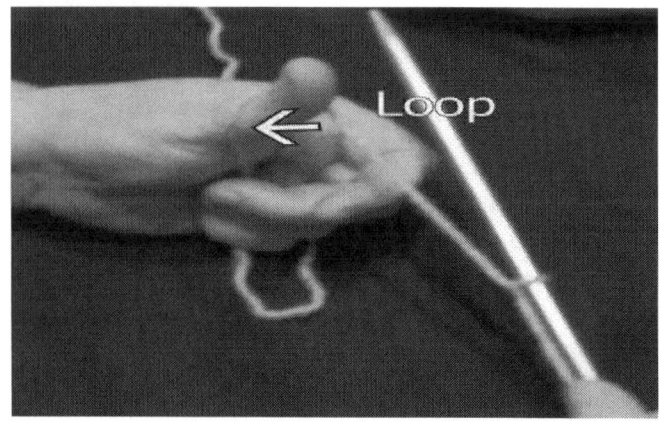

Illustration 21: Make a Loop

6. Insert the empty needle under the loop on the thumb and guide it to the back of the thumb holding the needle and skein end with the left-hand thumb and index finger.

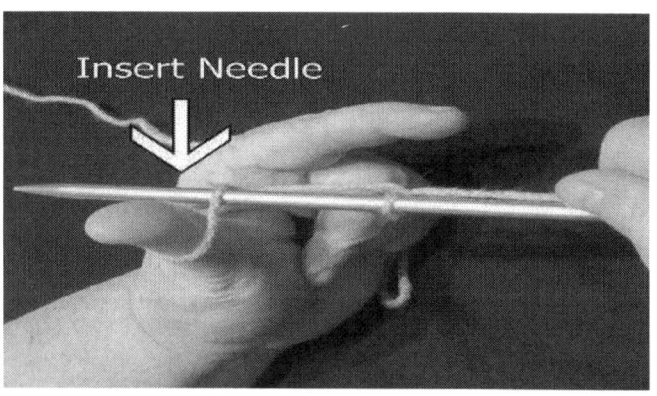

Illustration 22: Insert Receiving Needle

7. Take the 26-inch tail up from behind the left-hand thumb and wrap it around the tip of the needle.

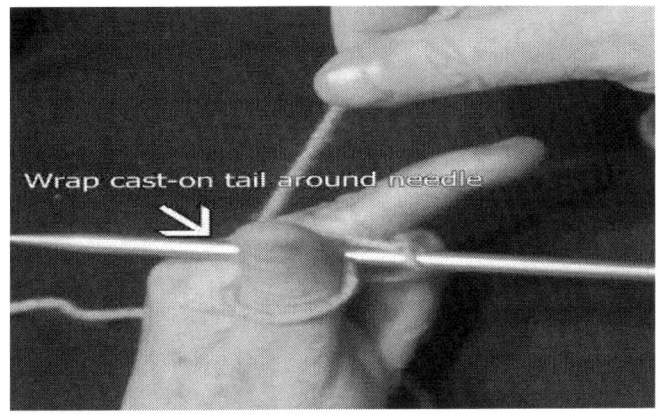

Illustration 23: Wrap Tail

8. Bring the 26-inch tail down and hold with right hand against the needle.
9. Move the needle downward with the right hand and poke through the thumb loop to bring it in front of the thumb.

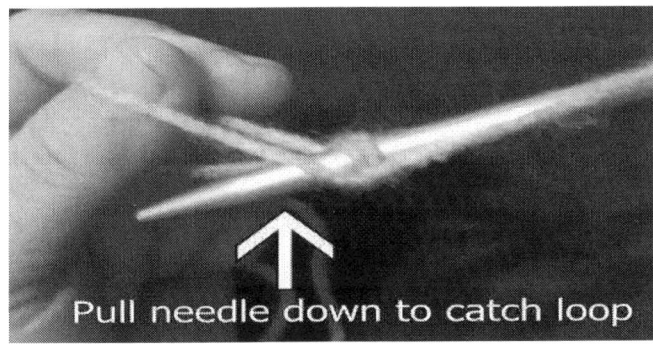

Illustration 24: Needle Through Loop

10. Hold 26-inch tail end with the right-hand thumb and index finger against the needle.

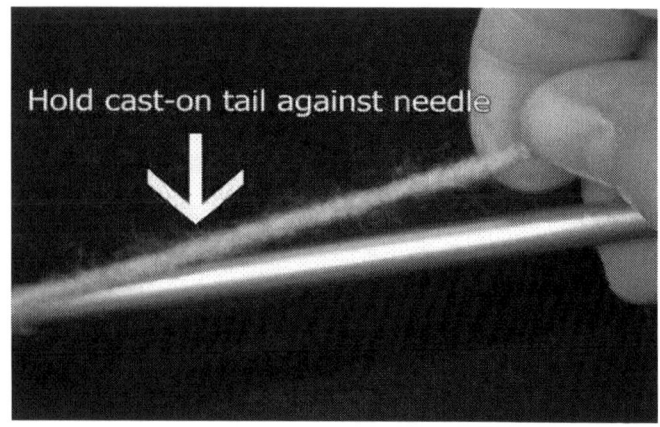

Illustration 25: Hold Tail

11. Release the thumb and pull the skein tail with the left-hand fingers to tighten the yarn around the needle, while stabilizing 26-inch tail with the right-hand thumb and index finger.

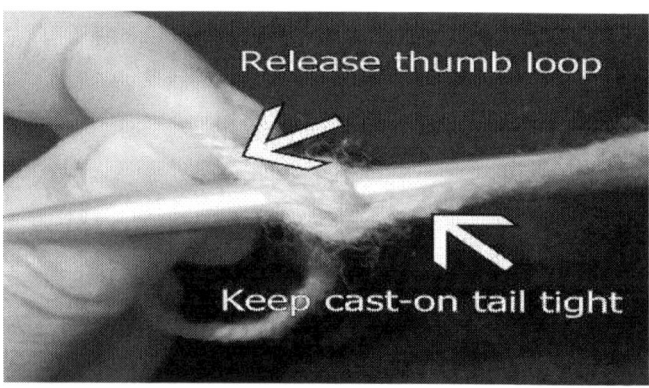

Illustration 26: Release Thumb

12. Keep the 26-inch tail, which will shorten with each stitch, to the right going toward the

stopper end of the needle and the skein tail going up toward the point of the needle.

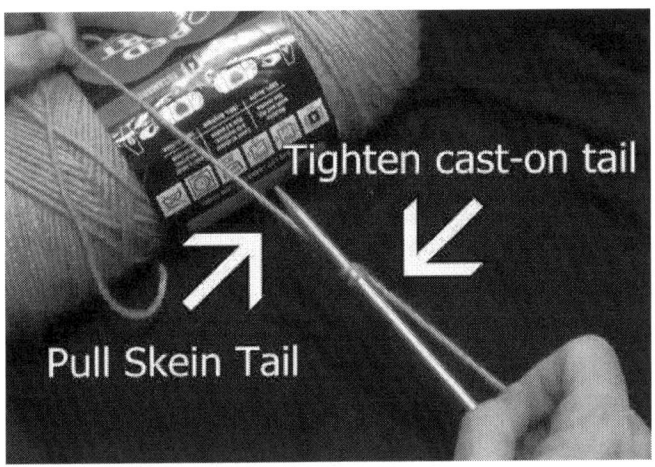

Illustration 27: Tail Position

13. Cast on, indicated by the abbreviation CO, 18 more stitches. When done 20 stitches will be on the needle. The slip knot counts as one stitch.

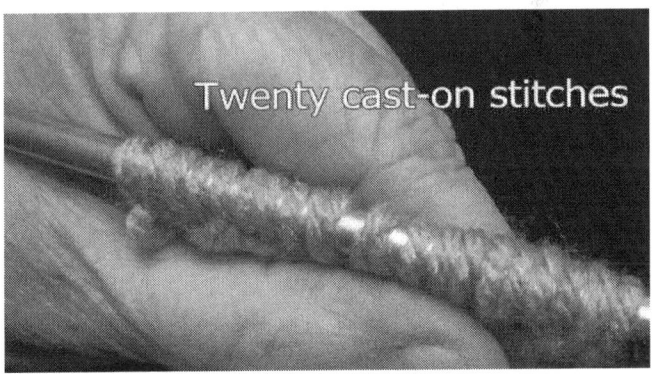

Illustration 28: Initial Stitches

Do not pull the tails too tight or it is impossible to insert the needles into the next row. Also do not keep them too loose or the weave will be uneven.

Note that an edge is developing at the bottom of the stitches. This is the bottom of the sampler.

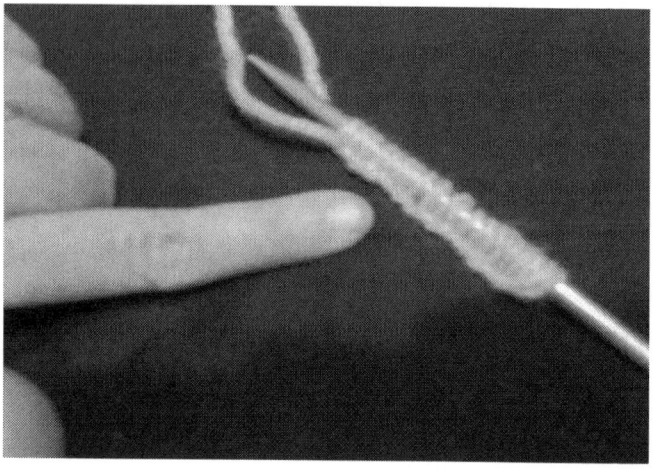

Illustration 29: Edge

Chapter 7: The Knit Stitch

The knit stitch is one of the two most important stitches to learn and the basis on which knitting is created.

To knit:

1. Hold the needle with the cast on stitches, or carrier needle in the left hand, bringing them up close to the tip of the needle, but not as far that they fall off.

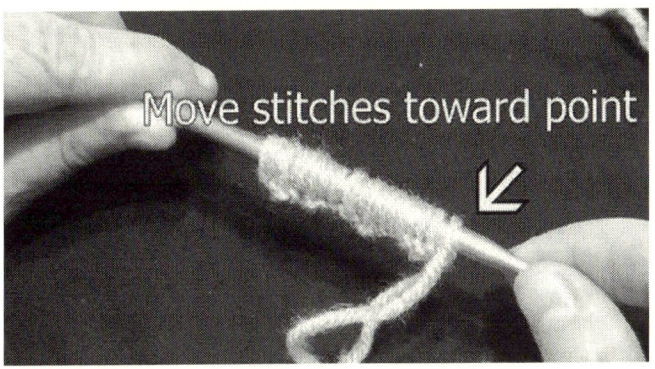

Illustration 30: Carrier Needle

2. Hold the empty needle, or receiving in the right hand between the thumb and index finger.

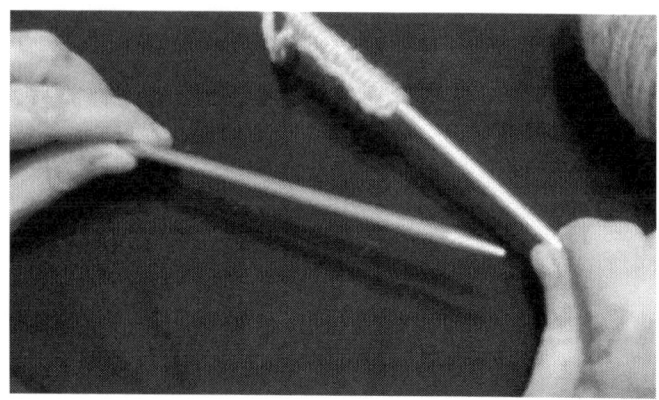

Illustration 31: Prepare to Knit

3. Insert the empty needle, or receiving needle, into the first cast on stitch and go under and behind the cast on needle.

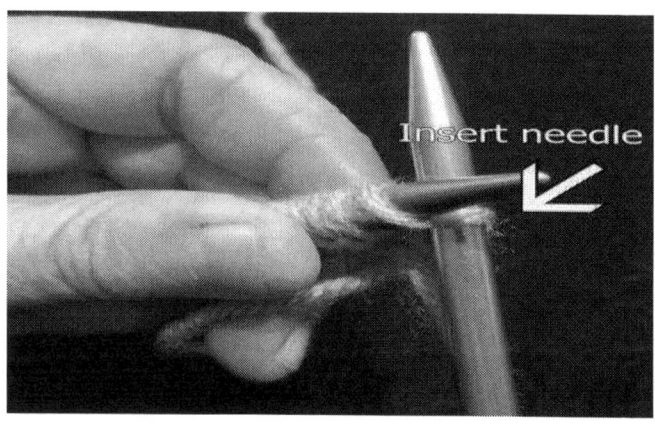

Illustration 32: Insert

TIP: Use the skein tail for all knitting now and ignore the tail that was once 26-inches long. Using the wrong tail will cause problems and the stitch will not be smooth. It will result in having to tear out all wrong stitches and re-knitting them.

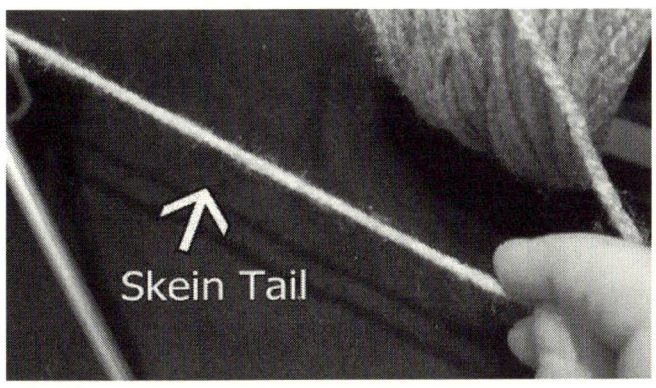

Illustration 33: Skein Tail

Illustration 34: Cast on Tail

4. Wrap the skein tail around, back to front - counter clockwise, over the empty needle and pull with the right thumb and finger.

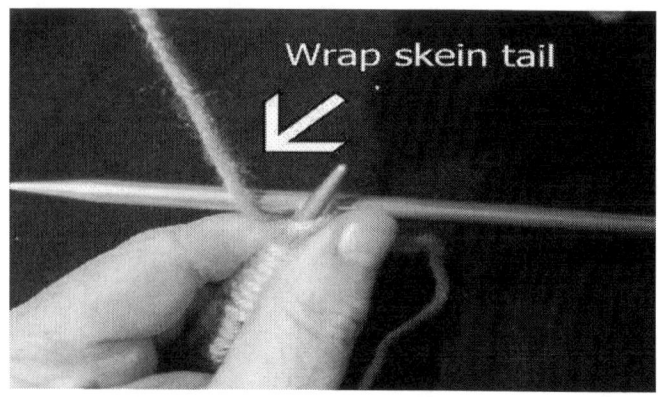

Illustration 35: Wrap Counter Clockwise

5. Hold needles in an "X" shape with the left thumb and index finger.

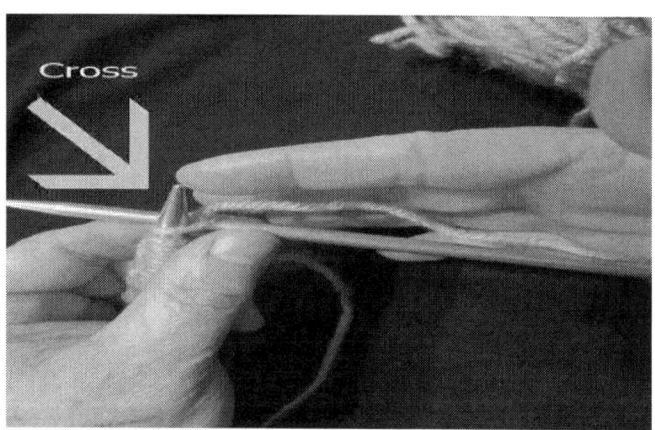

Illustration 36: "X" Configuration

6. Grip the skein tail and empty needle with the right-hand fingers and slide the needle down.

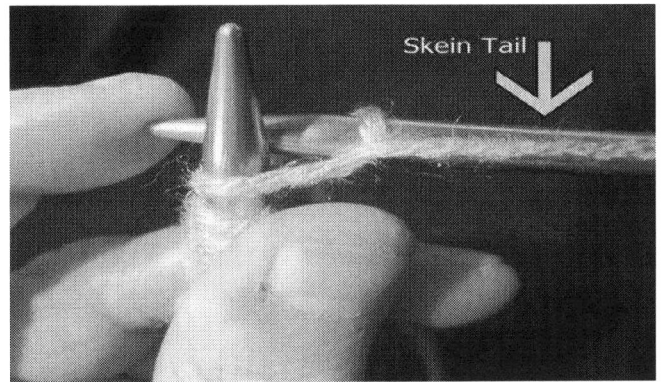

Illustration 37: Skein Tail Knit Position

7. Keep the index finger of the left hand against the tip of the empty needle to guide it up through the loop of yarn to the front of the Cast On needle.

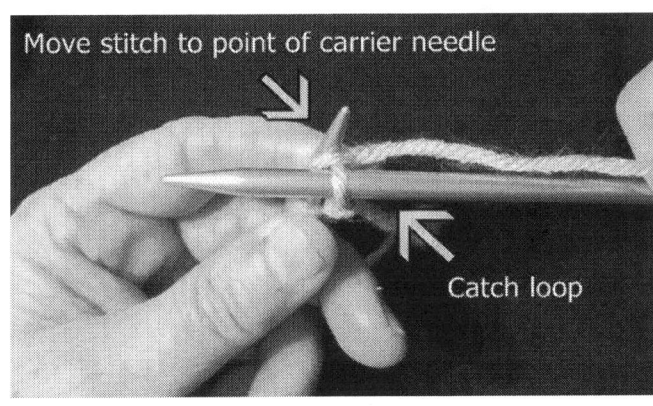

Illustration 38: Guide Tip Through Loop

8. Pull the stitch toward the pointed end of the needle.

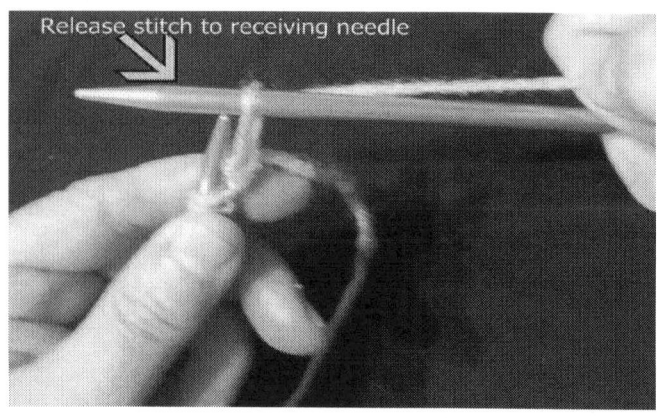

Illustration 39: Release to Receiving Needle

9. Draw only one stitch off the end of the needle

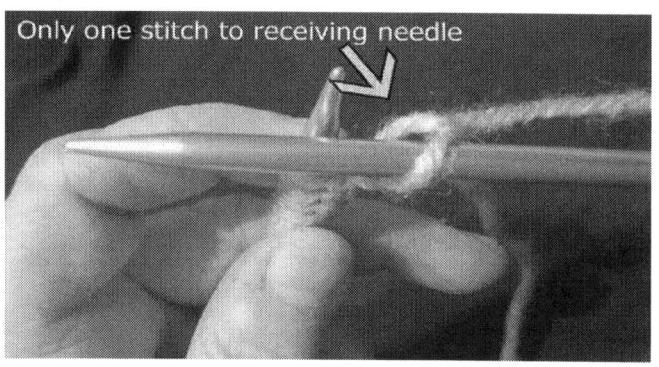

Illustration 40: Move One Stitch

10. Pull tight. There is now one stitch on the receiving needle and 19 stitches on the cast on needle.

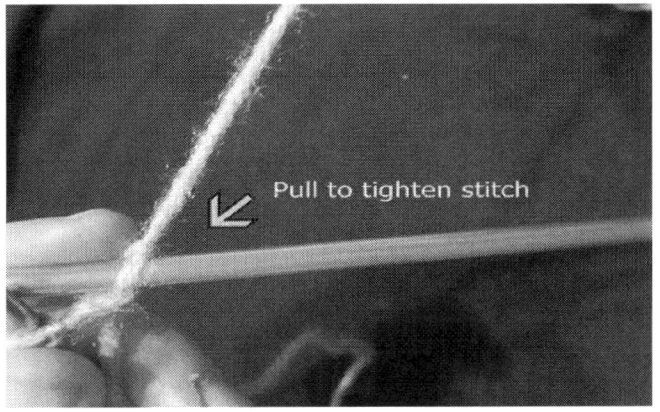

Illustration 41: One Knit Stitch

11. Keep the skein tail to the back of the receiving needle before trying to make the next stitch. When doing a knit stitch, the tail must always be to the back of the work.

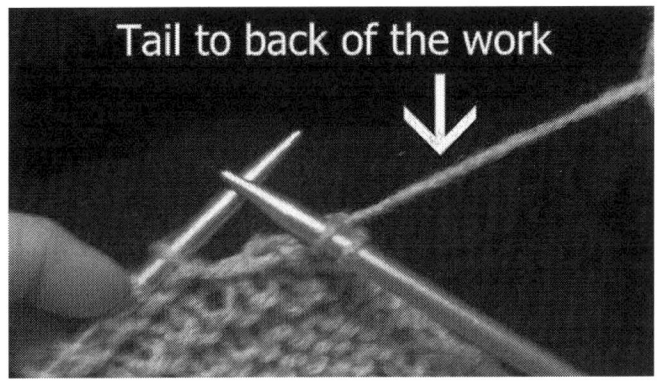

Illustration 42: Skein Tail to Purl Position

12. Do the same with the rest of the 19 stitches.
13. Practice by knitting 10 rows.

14. Use the left thumb and index finger to stabilize stitches as they transfer to the receiving needle. Do not pull so tight it is hard to insert needles into the next row. Notice how the work is smooth under the knit row. It will not be smooth when doing the next stitch.

Chapter 8: The Purl Stitch

The purl stitch is a little different from the knit stitch and once mastered, it allows the knitter to make different patterns in their work.

To purl:

1. Hold the needle with the stitches on it, the carrier needle in the left hand and the empty needle, or receiving needle in the right hand

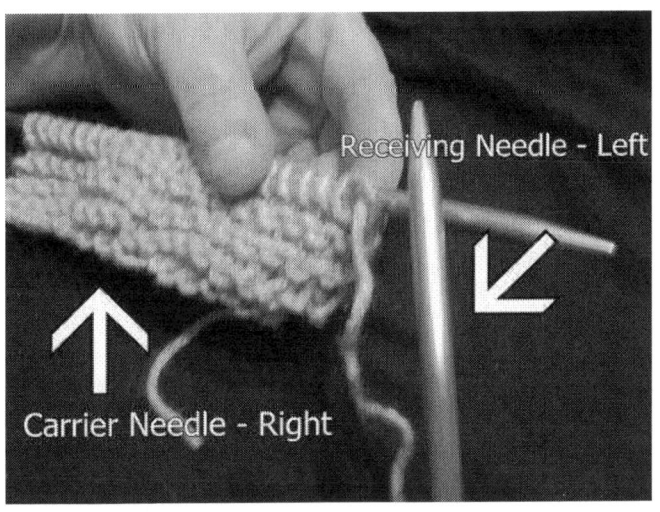

Illustration 43: Needle Positions

2. Insert the point of the empty needle in the first stitch on the other needle by guiding it through the stitch from top to bottom, or downward.

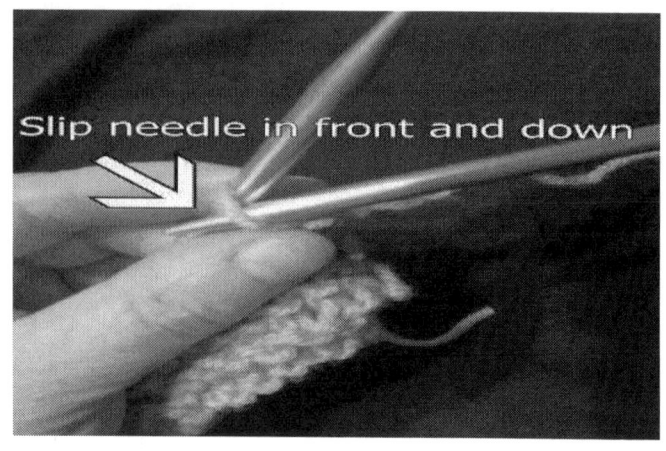

Illustration 44: Insert

3. IMPORTANT - The skein tail should be in the front of the needles. When knitting it is at the back.

Illustration 45: Tail Position

4. Bring the skein tail up around the back of the empty needle point and around to the front in a counter clockwise motion.

IMPORTANT: Always wrap yarn around the needle in a counter clockwise manner. Wrapping any other way will cause extra stitches to be on the needle and holes will appear in the project.

Illustration 46: Wrap Tail

5. Bring the empty needle, or receiving needle, down and push with the left-hand thumb so it catches a loop.

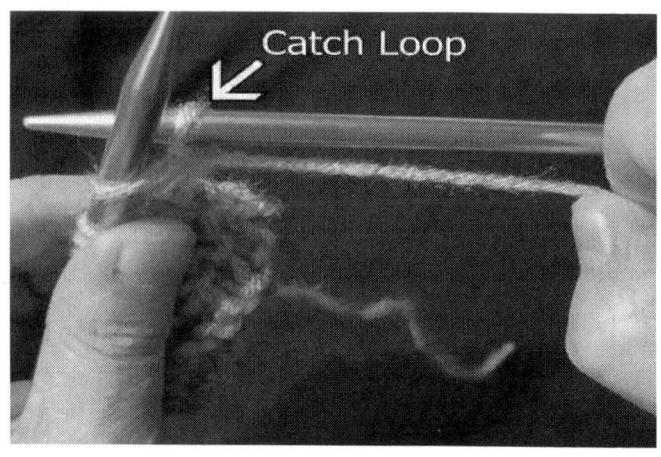

Illustration 47: Catch Loop

6. Ease the first stitch off the full carrier needle onto the empty receiving needle.

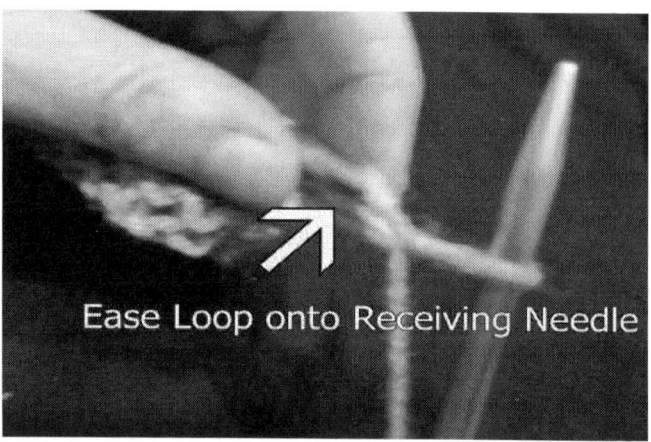

Illustration 48: Transfer to Receiving Needle

7. Pull lightly on the skein tail to snug the knot.

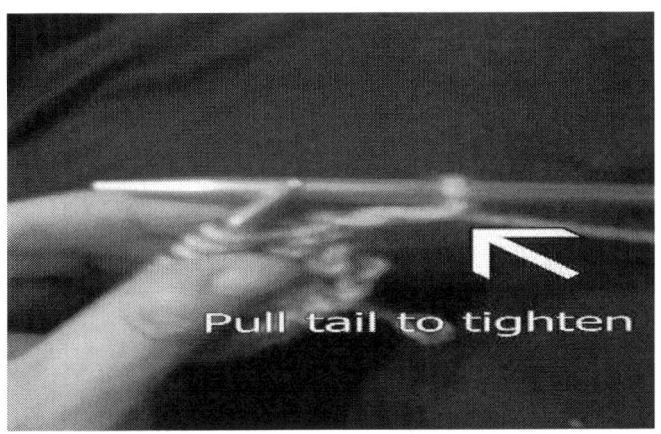

Illustration 49: Tighten

8. Continue doing the same with the 19 other stitches on the carrier needle. Make sure the skein tail is always to the front when purling (in knitting it is to the back).

Illustration 50: Purl Stitches

9. Look at a purl row and notice under each stitch there is a little bump. When knitting, this area is smooth. This is how you can tell which stitch each row has.

Illustration 51: Bumps

Illustration 52: Smooth

Practice by completing 10 purl rows on the sampler.

Chapter 9: How to Increase Stitches

Increase stitches add to the total stitches on a needle in order to widen the project. Several techniques are used to do an increase including a plain increase indicated with the abbreviation inc, or the yarn over technique indicated by the abbreviation yo.

To make an increase stitch:

1. Knit a stitch, but instead of sliding the stitch over to the receiving needle, leave it on the carrying needle and stretch it out a little.

Illustration 53: Slip Knitwise

2. Move the point of the receiving needle behind the carrying needle.

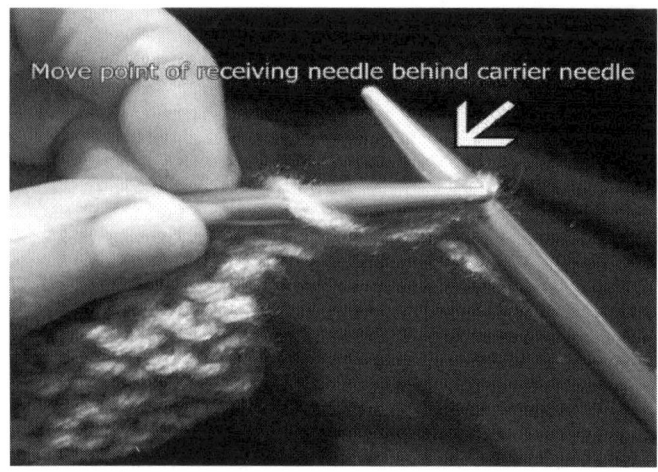

Illustration 54: Move Point

3. Insert the tip of the receiving needle in the back of the same first knitted stich that was left on the needle.

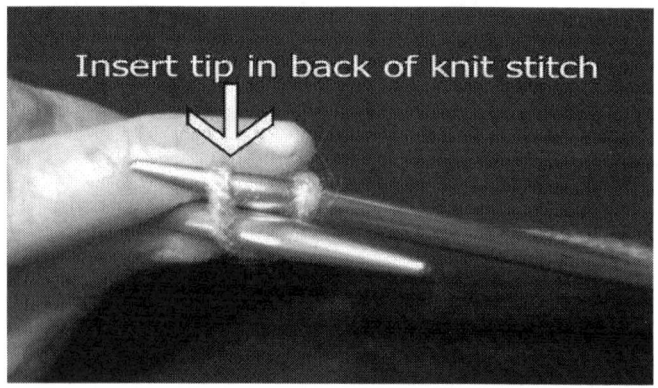

Illustration 55: Insert

4. Wrap the skein tail around the tip of the receiving needle from back to front.

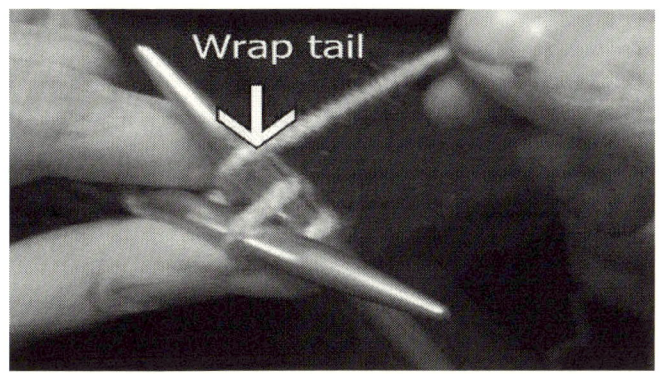

Illustration 56: Wrap

5. Guide the needle with the left-hand thumb and index finger through to catch the loop and bring it up.

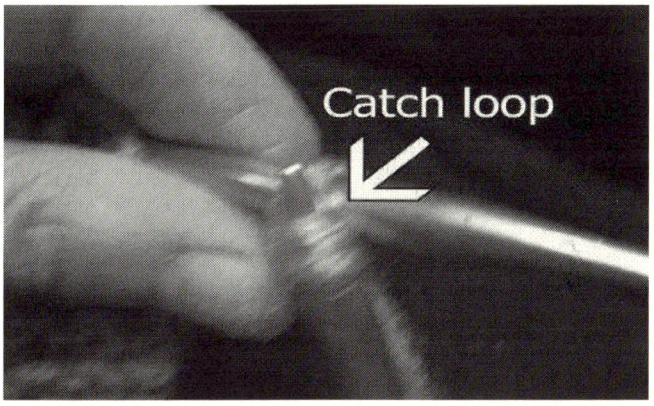

Illustration 57: Catch

6. Slide the stitch over from the carrier needle to the receiving needle.

Illustration 58: Slide

Tip: Hold the skein tail very taunt in order to transfer the stitch easily.

    7. Tighten the stitch slightly by pulling on the skein tail and one stitch is now two.

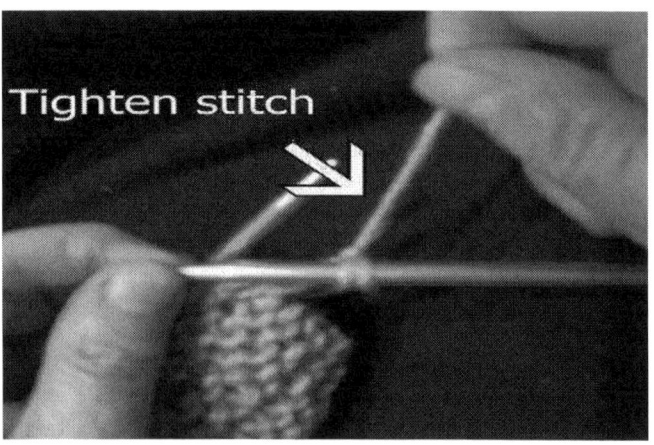

Illustration 59: Tighten

On the sampler do the following:

- Knit the first stitch
- Increase on the 2nd stitch
- Knit up to the 18th stitch
- Increase again
- Knit the last stitch and turn

There should now be 22 stitches on the sample needle.

Illustration 60: Sampler

Knit 5 more rows.

Yarn Over Increase

Another way to increase stitches on a project is to perform a yarn over. To do a yarn over proceed with the following:

8. Knit one stitch.

Illustration 61: Knit

9. Move the tail from back to front as if going to purl, but instead knit another stitch.

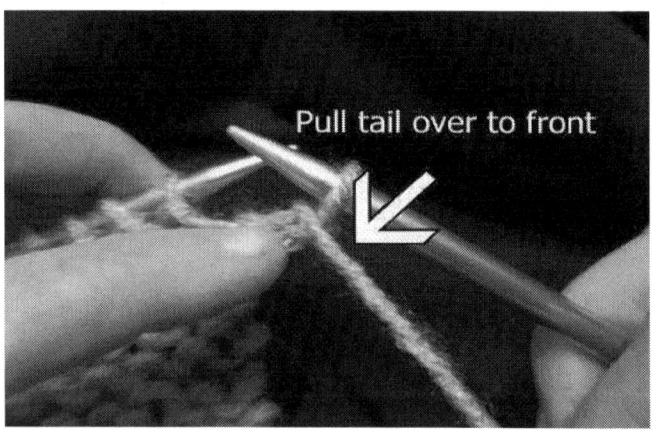

Illustration 62: Move Tail

Look at the receiving needle and see that there are now three stitches on the needle instead of just two

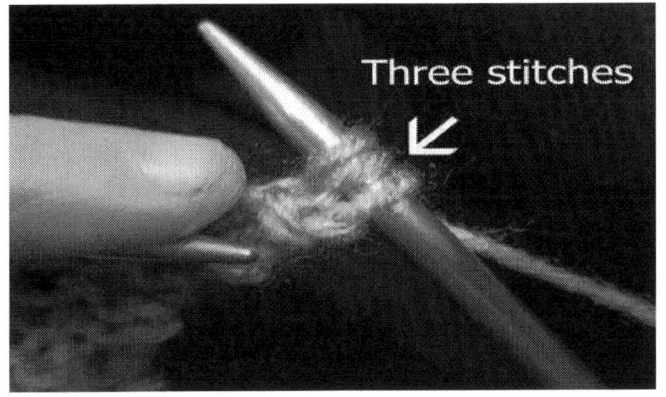

Illustration 63: Stitches

10. Knit 19 stitches on the sample, yarn over, and knit the last stitch. There are now 24 stitches on the receiving needle.

The yarn over stitch tends to twist into the previous stitch. Always take the time to separate it from the first stitch before moving on to make it a distinct added stitch.

Increases and yarn overs are possible to do when doing a purl row. Just purl instead of knit and yarn over to the back instead of the front. These stitches are most often performed in a knit row simply because it makes it a little easier.

Chapter 10: How to Decrease Stitches

Just as increasing adds stitches to a project, decreasing takes stitches away and the project becomes narrower. The abbreviation for decrease is dec. Use the following instructions on the sampler to decrease stitches.

Decreasing during a Knit row:

1. Knit the first stitch on the sampler.

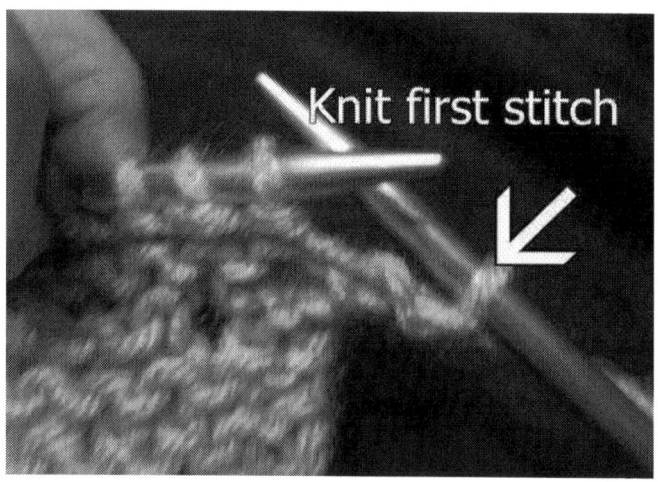

Illustration 64: Knit

2. Knit two stitches together by inserting the tip of the receiving needle into the next two stitches on the carrier needle.

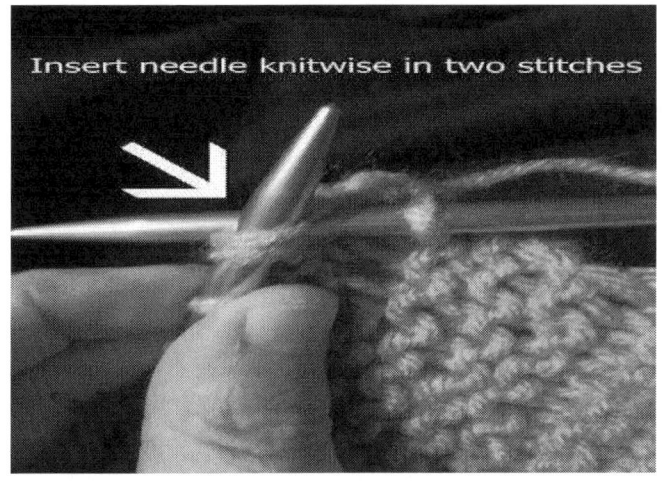

Illustration 65: Insert

3. Knit the two stitches together to make one stitch. This is sometimes abbreviated in a pattern as k2tog.

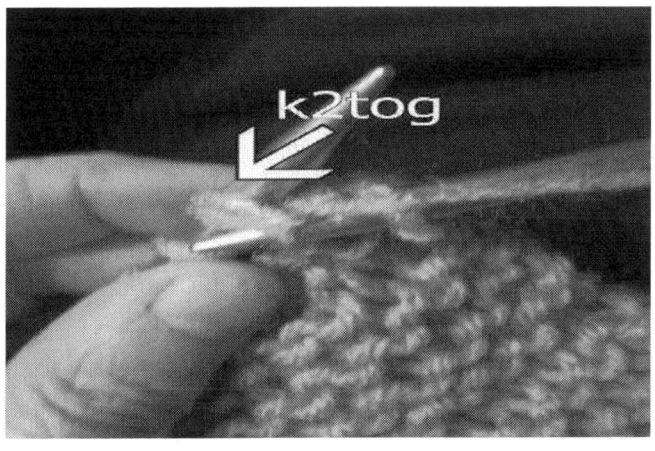

Illustration 66: Knit Together

Knit 6 rows on the sampler.

Decreasing during a Purl Row:

Decreasing while purling is very similar to doing it in a knit row.

4. Purl 1 stitch on the sampler.

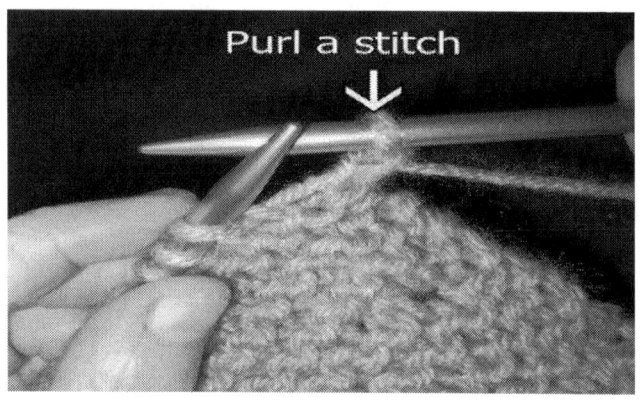

Illustration 67: Purl

5. Purl two stitches together by inserting the tip of the receiving needle down through the front of the next two stitches on the carrier needle.

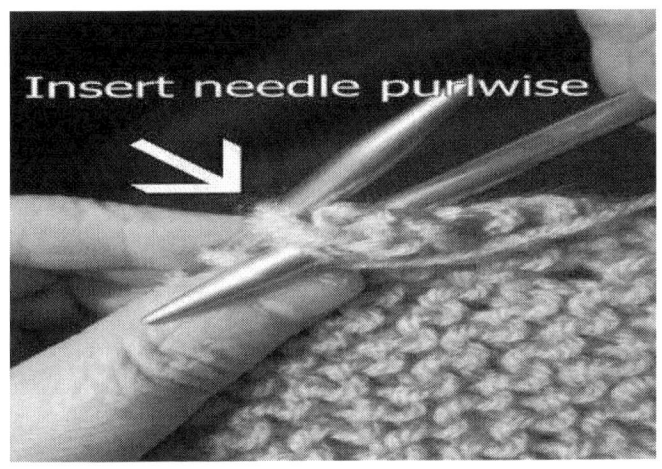

Illustration 68: Insert

6. Bring the skein tail up and over the tip of the receiving needle to purl the stitch.

Illustration 69: Wrap

7. Purl on the sampler until there are only three stitches on the carrier needle. Perform a purl two together decrease with the first two stitches

and purl the last stitch. This is often called p2tog.

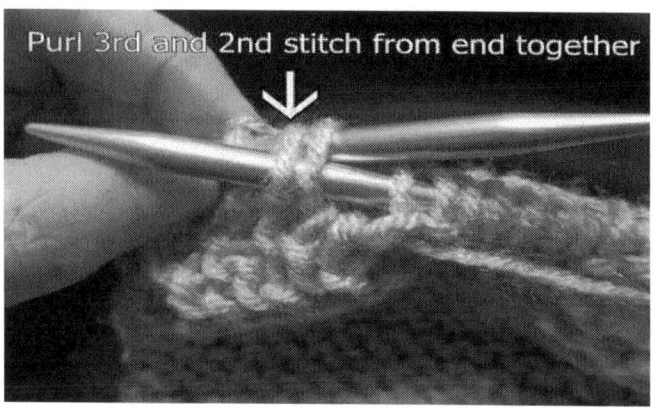

Illustration 70: Purl b

8. Purl the last stitch on the needle.

Purl 6 rows on the sampler.

PSSO

Another way to decrease stitches is to slip a stitch, knit and pass the slip stitch over. It sounds confusion, but is actually very easy and keeps all the stitches in a project tight and tidy. This type of decrease is indicated in a pattern by the abbreviation psso, meaning pass slip stitch over.

9. Knit one stitch on the sampler.

Illustration 71: Knit

10. Slip one stitch from the carrier needle unto the receiving needle without knitting or purling. Just slip it over by inserting the tip of the receiving needle, as if to knit, and move it over to the receiving needle.

Illustration 72: Slip

There should be one knit stitch and one slipped stitch on the receiving needle.

11. Knit the next stitch as you would any other knit stitch.

Illustration 73: Knit

12. Insert the tip of the carrier needle into the slipped stitch on the receiving needle.

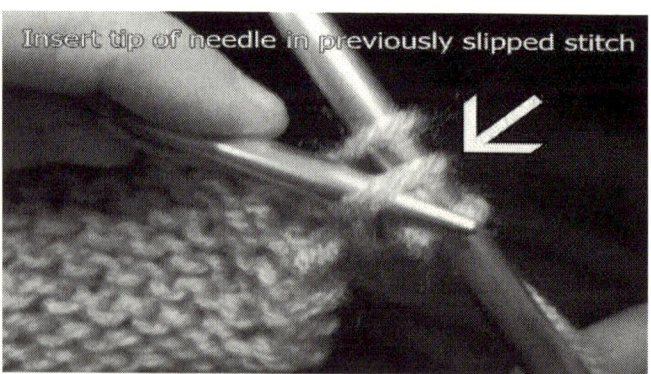

Illustration 74: Insert

13. Hold the skein tail tight and pull the slipped stitch backwards over the last over the last knitted stitch on the receiving needle.

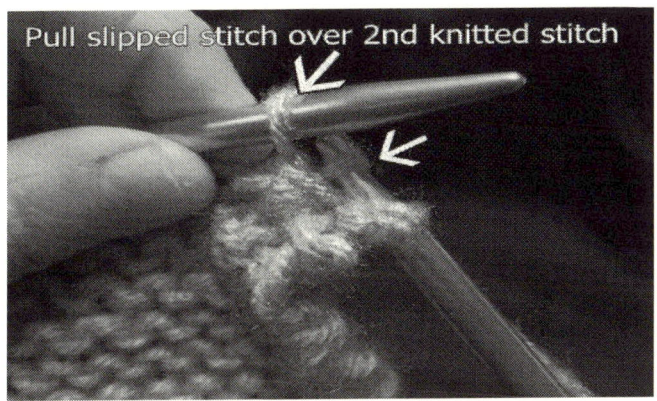

Illustration 75: Pull

14. Slide the stitch over the tip of the needle and let fall leaving only the knitted stitch on the needle. Pull the skein tail to tighten the stitch.

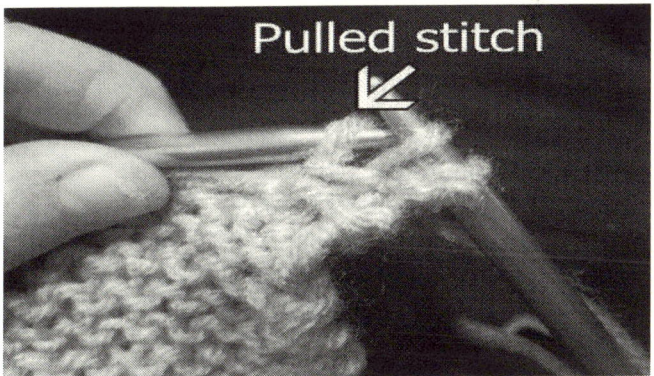

Illustration 76: Slip

15. Knit on the sampler until only 4 stitches remain on the carrier needle.

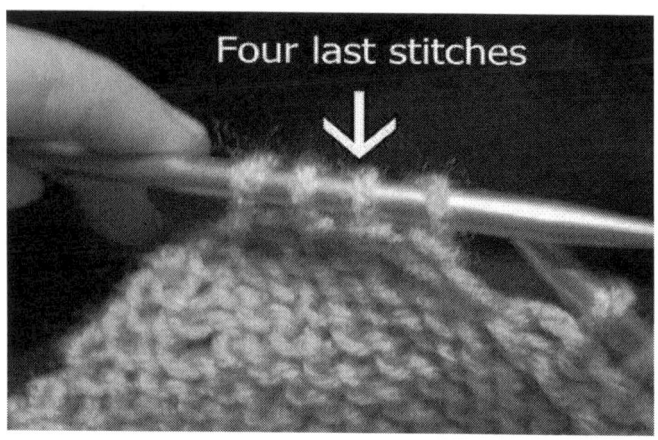

Illustration 77: Stitches on Needle

16. Slip the stitch over from the carrier to the receiving needle, knit the next stitch and slip the slip stitch over to fall and tighten by pulling on the tail.

On the sampler, practice all the increase and decrease methods. Start by doing an increase method over the entire row then do a decrease method over the next.

Chapter 11: How to Join Yarn

Joining one end of yarn to another is necessary when changing color of yarn within a pattern, or when attaching another skein when the first one runs out.

Always attach yarn at the end or beginning of a row. Attaching anywhere else puts an unsightly bump in the pattern.

To Join:

1. Tie a loose single knot in the new yarn making sure to leave a 4-inch tail that is woven into the work later. Do not tighten the knot.

Illustration 78: Knot

2. Insert the tail of the old yarn into the knot leaving at least a 4-inch tail.

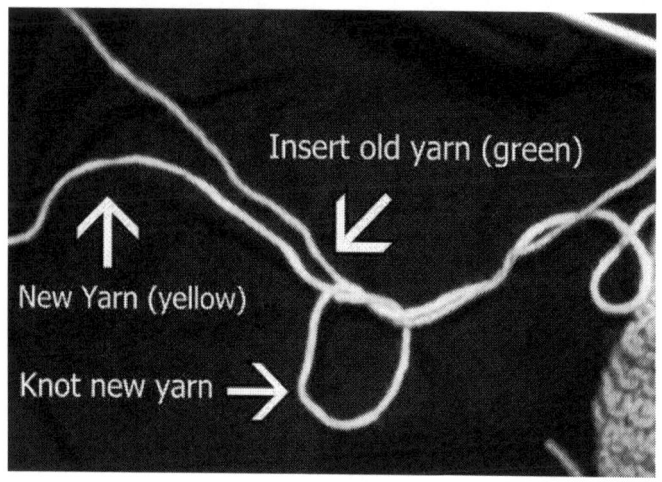

Illustration 79: Insert Old Yarn

3. Move the knot close to the edge of the work.

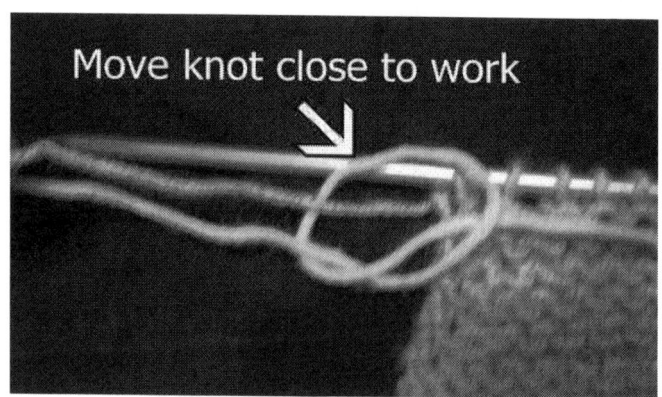

Illustration 80: Move Knot

4. Snug the knot, but don't make it so tight you can never get it out.

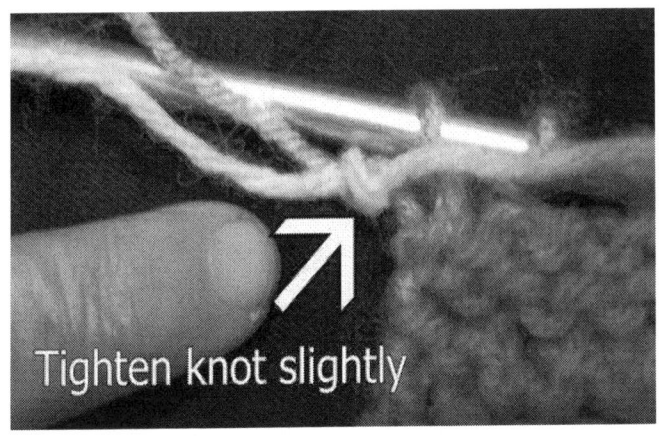

Illustration 81: Tighten Knot

Two tails will sit at the edge of the work. One is from the old yarn and one is from the new yarn. Avoid catching them into the next rows while working them. Either weave them into the work immediately or wait until the project is completed and do all the weaving. To see how to weave go to the chapter on finishing.

Color changes in a pattern, where yarn may have to be joined, are identified by the abbreviations MC as the Main color or CC as contrasting color. A striped scarf would have two colors. Red may be the main color and white would be the contrasting color or vice versa. Each color section could be 10 rows wide and the yarn joins at the edge of every 10 rows.

The reason the joining knot is not snugged tight is because during finishing, it is untied and woven into the work. This way it does not leave an unsightly bulge in the work.

Chapter 12: Binding Off

Binding off is the process of ending a project. It seals the stitches and takes them off the needle.

To Bind Off:

1. Knit two stitches.

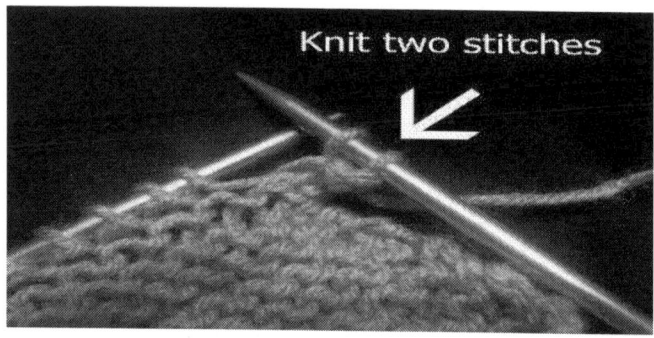

Illustration 82: Knit

2. Insert tip of the carrier needle into the first knit stitch on the receiving needle as if going to knit.

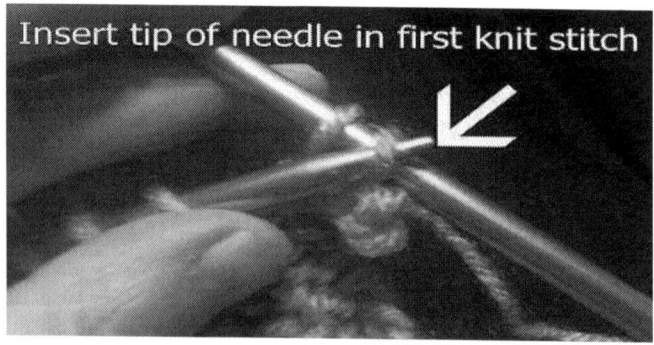

Illustration 83: Insert Tip

3. Pull and stretch the first knit stitch. Stretch it over the second stitch.

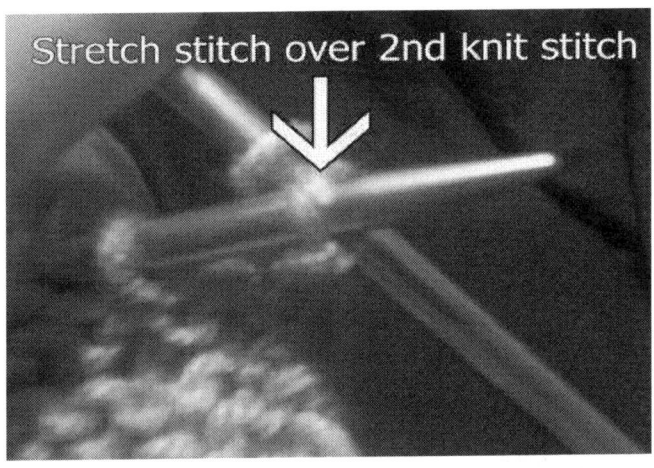

Illustration 84: Stretch

4. Pull stretched stitch over the tip of the receiving needle.

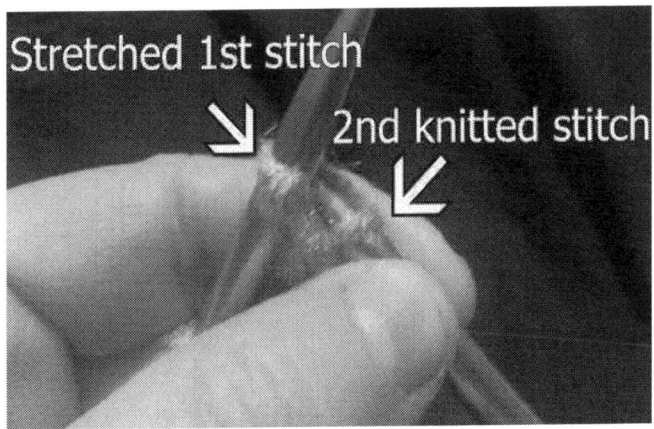

Illustration 85: Pull Off

5. Let stretched stitch fall off the needle.

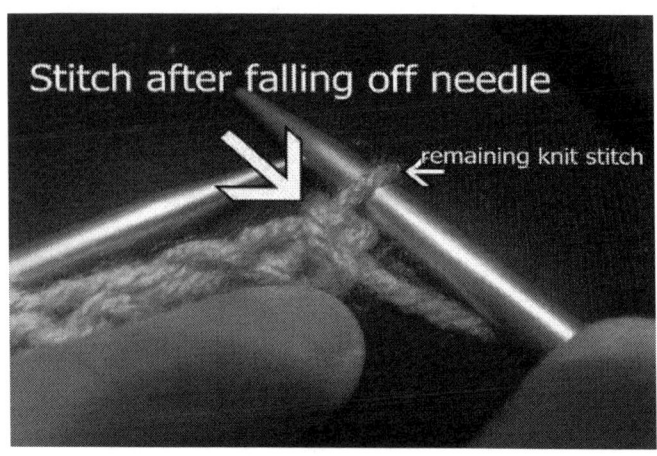

Illustration 86: Let Fall

6. Only one stitch should be on the receiving needle at this time. Knit another stitch to make two stitches on the receiving needle.

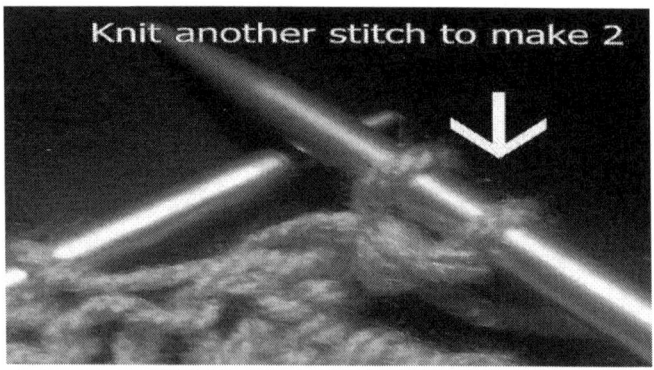

Illustration 87: Knit Second Stitch

7. Insert tip of needle and stretch stitch over previous stitch again.

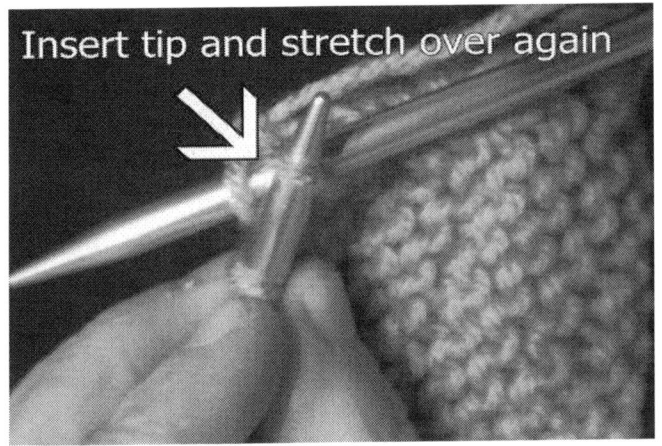

Illustration 88: Insert and Stretch

8. Bring stitch over the needle and let it fall.

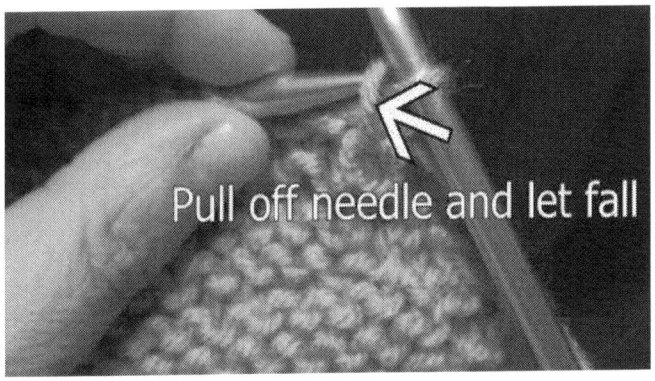

Illustration 89: Let Fall

9. Continue with rest of stitches. There should only be one or two stitches on the receiving needle at any time. An ending edge will form.

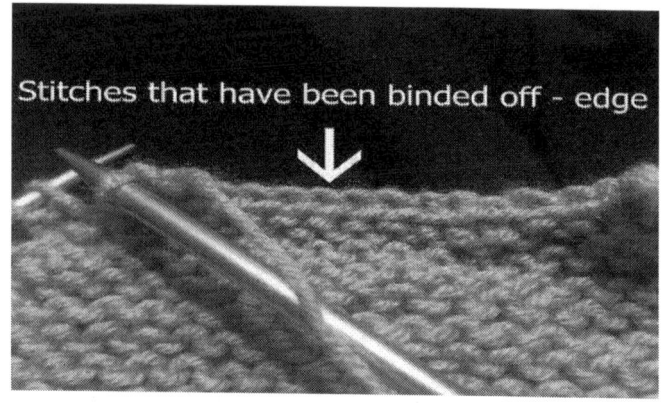

Illustration 90: Edge

10. Stop when there is only one last stitch left on the carrier needle. Knit that stitch.

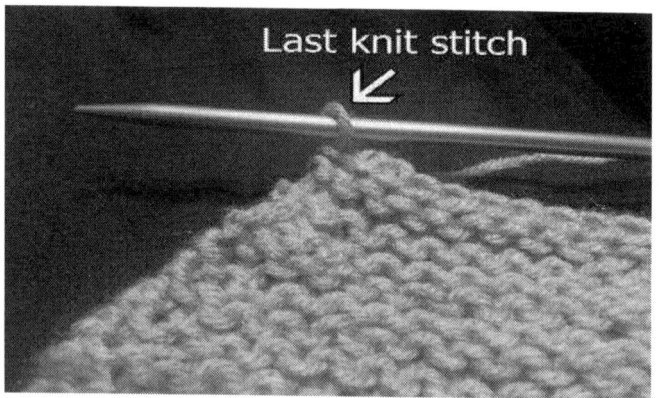

Illustration 91: One Stitch Left

11. Pull needle up making a long loop.

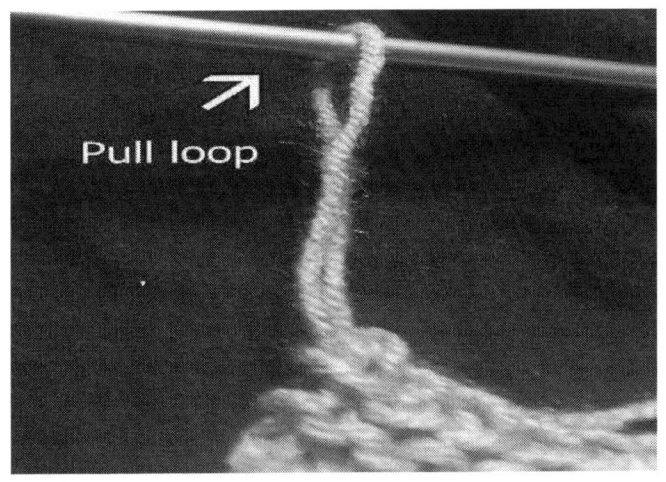

Illustration 92: Pull

12. Cut the yarn leaving a 3-inch long tail.

Illustration 93: Cut

13. Pull the loop all the way through to lock stitches in and pull tight.

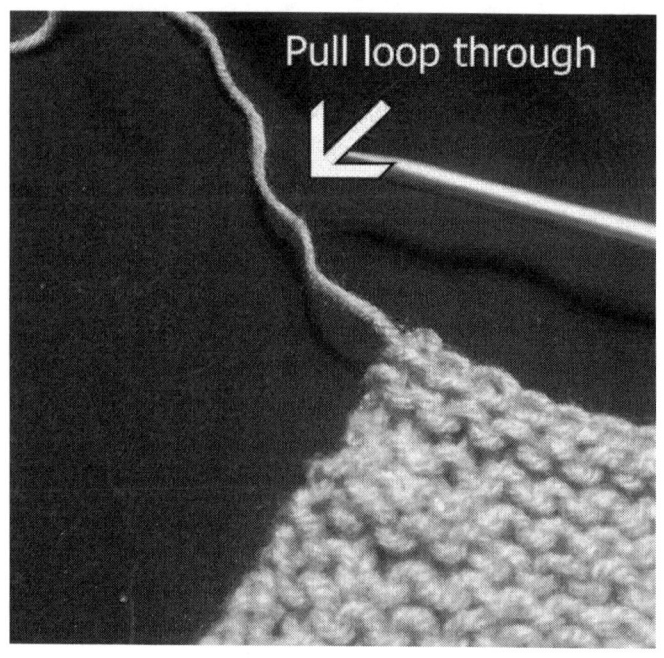

Illustration 94: Pull

Weave the tail into the project as per instructions in Finishing Chapter.

Binding off is sometimes called casting off.

Binding off is abbreviated bo and casting off is abbreviated co

Binding off stops any unraveling and ends the project.

Try not to pull too tight on the yarn while binding off. If that happens, the top edge will pucker. If this seems to be a problem, use a carrier needle two sizes larger from the receiving needle.

Chapter 13: How to Finish A Project

Finishing a piece the right way can often make a big difference in the quality of the project. Loose strings are a dead give-away that the knitter really did not do a good job. It is very important to weave in all those little tails so they can no longer be seen frin tge right side of the project. It is fine if little tails are exposed on the wrong side, as long as they are not too long.

One Color Vertical Weave

The first method of finishing a project is to weave vertically down the edge of a piece. This works best if the project has several different pieces that are stitched together. The seam hides the finishing weave. A good example is a sweater that has a body piece and two sleeve pieces. Sewing the sleeves into the body hides the finishing weaves at the seams where it cannot be seen. Sewing the side seams will also hide the tail weaving.

1. Thread the tail into a blunt, large eye needle made for yarn and knitting projects.

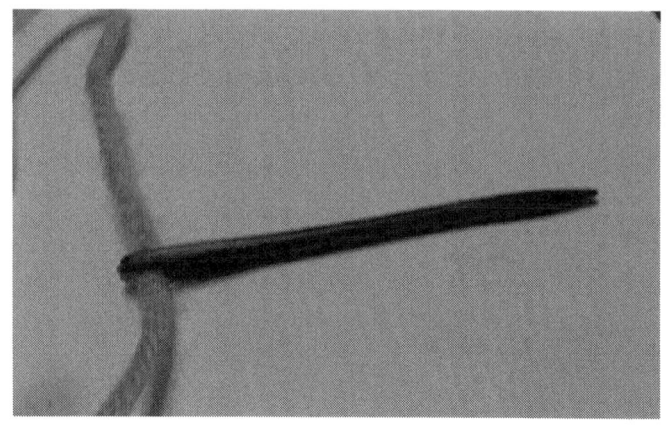

Illustration 95: Thread

2. On the wrong side, or side that lies against the body or inside, weave the needle down five to six side loops.

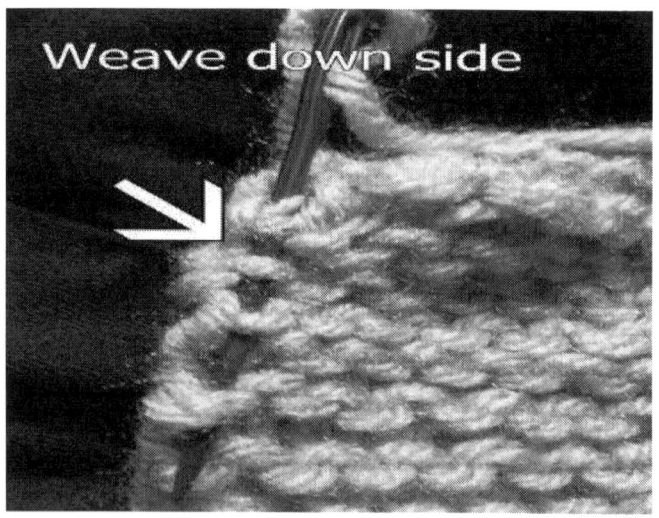

Illustration 96: Weave

3. Take a small stitch in the side of the project and pull the yarn into a single knot.

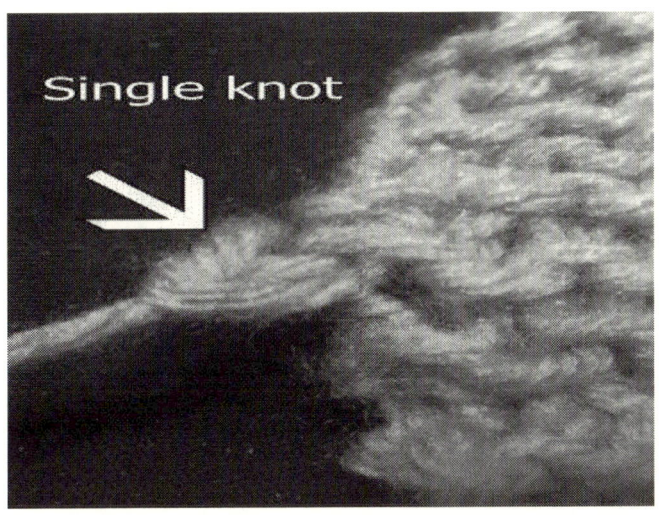

Illustration 97: Stitch and Knot

4. Knot once more and cut the excess yarn leaving just a small tail.

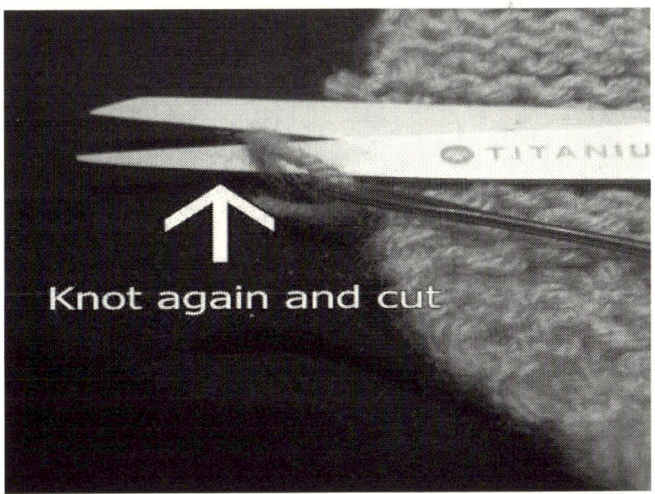

Illustration 98: Knot and Cut

One Color Horizontal Weave

Weaving horizontally through the piece is another way of finishing a project. Always weave on the wrong side of the piece so it does not show on the front.

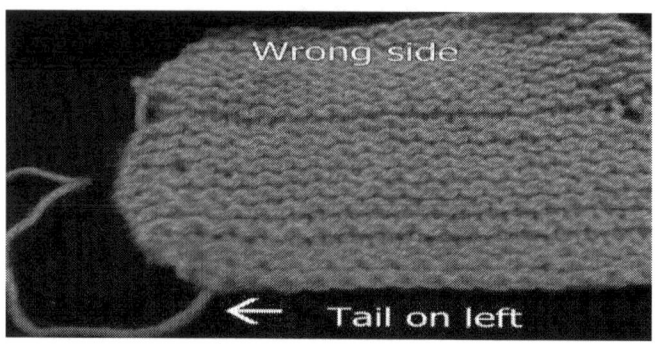

Illustration 99: Finish Wrong Side

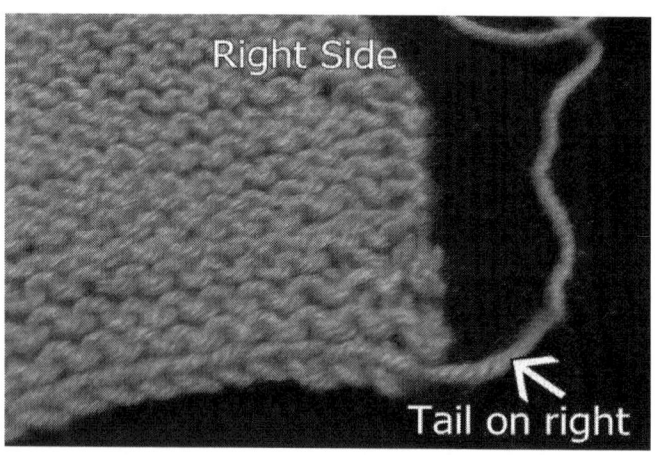

Illustration 100: Right Side of Project

5. Thread the tail into a blunt, large eye needle made for yarn and knitting projects.

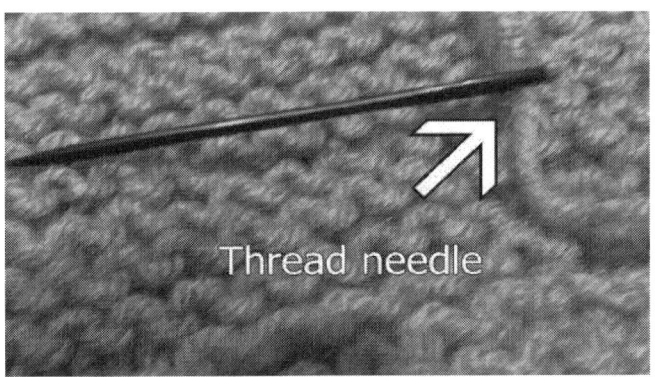

Illustration 101: Thread

6. Weave the needle through five to eight stitches horizontally going in and out. End on the wrong side of the piece.

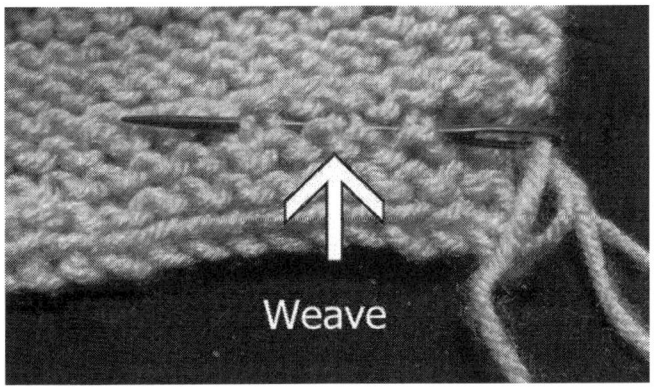

Illustration 102: Weave

7. Never knot because it will show through in the garment and make a big lump.

Snip the tail off close to the work, but not so close it will work out to the front.

Two Color Vertical Weave

When two colors are used to make a striped pattern there are two tails to weave from where the two different colors of yarn were joined. To do a vertical weave just take one tail and go up and the other and weave down.

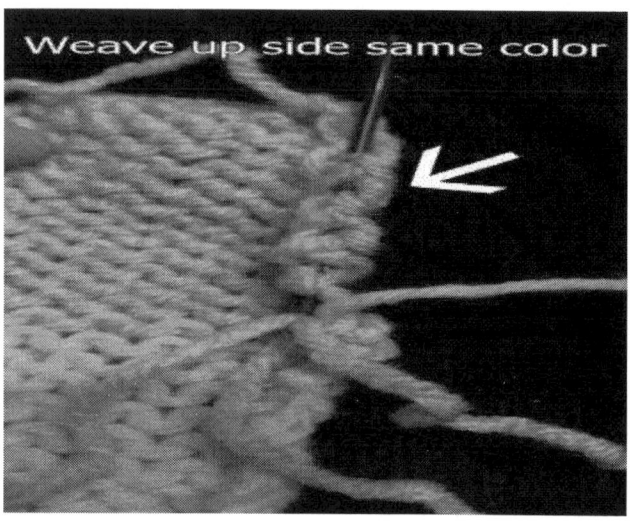

Illustration 103: Vertical One Color

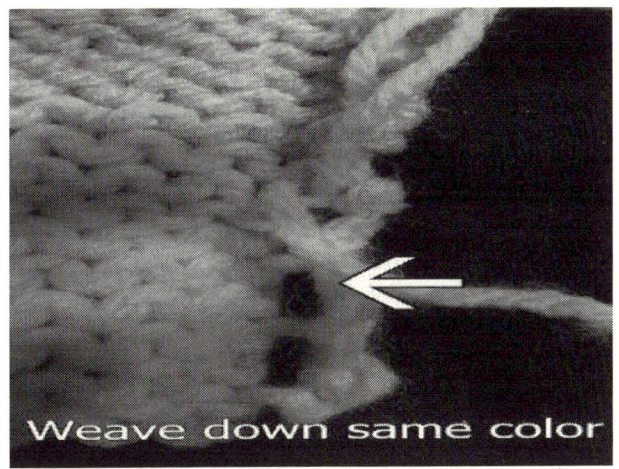

Illustration 104: Vertical Second Color

Two Color Horizontal Weave

To do a horizontal weave take one tail and weave horizontally at the edge of the same color and then do the other color at the edge of its color.

Illustration 105: Horizontal One Color

Illustration 106: Horizontal Second Color

Chapter 14: Blocking

Some knitters will insist that blocking is unnecessary but when done correctly, final project is polished and perfect when it is blocked. Blocking is the process of molding a knitted project into shape and making sure each side is straight and even. A sweater that has one sleeve shorter than the other or one side of the cardigan is longer than the other has never been blocked. Blocking a project makes everything even.

Check the yarn label before blocking to see the recommended blocking method to use for that yarn. Blocking is a little different for acrylic yarn than it is for wool yarn.

Block a project that has only one piece right after it is finished, like a scarf. Block a long project in sections. Block projects that have more than one piece, like a sweater, before the pieces are sewn together. Block all pieces of the project at the same time.

Block synthetic yarns including acrylic, rayon and nylon as follows:

Wet Blocking Method

1. Place a clean dish towel in a bowl of water and soak for about 5 to 8 minutes.

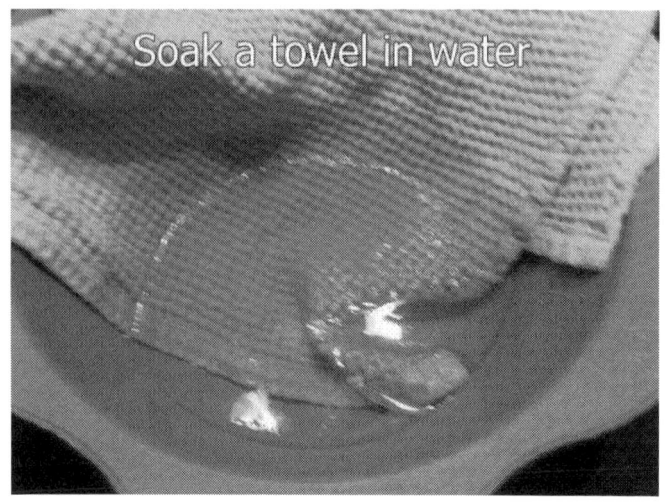

Illustration 107: Soak

2. Place the project, wrong side up, on a flat board covered with a few bath towels. Use an ironing board covered with towels or cut a piece of plywood cut sits comfortably on top of the clothes drier.

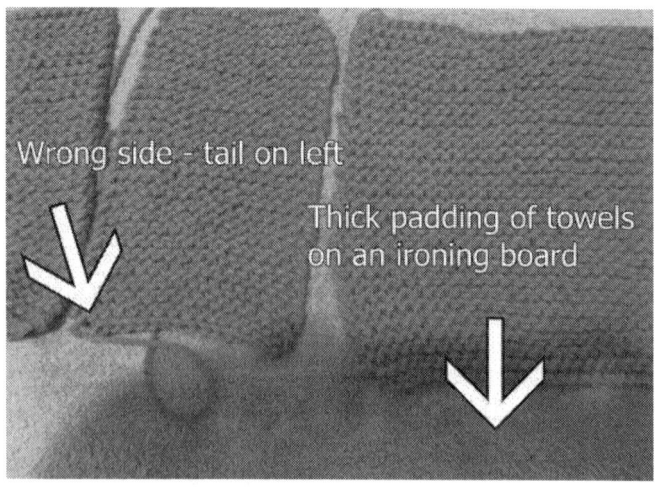

Illustration 108: Wrong Side

3. Stretch the project out into the final shape. Use a tape measure to make sure each side is even and check the rows to be certain they are straight.

Illustration 109: Blocked Correctly

Illustration 110: Blocked Incorrectly

4. If the project will not lie straight, use rust proof pins to keep it straight pushing them into the towels below. Avoid pins with plastic colored heads as they will sometimes melt using certain blocking methods.

Illustration 111: Pin

5. Wring the dish towel out so that it is still wet but not dripping and lay it over top of the project. Use several towels if necessary or block in sections.

6. Leave the project alone until it is completely dry. It might take more than 24 hours and up to two whole days. Do not even move the dish towel.

Spray Blocking

Another method of wet blocking uses a spray bottle instead of a wet dish cloth.

1. Lay the project wrong side up on the board and measure, tug and pin into shape.

Illustration 113: Lay Out and Pin

2. Fill a clean spray bottle with cool water. Spray generously on the project so that it is wet but not dripping.

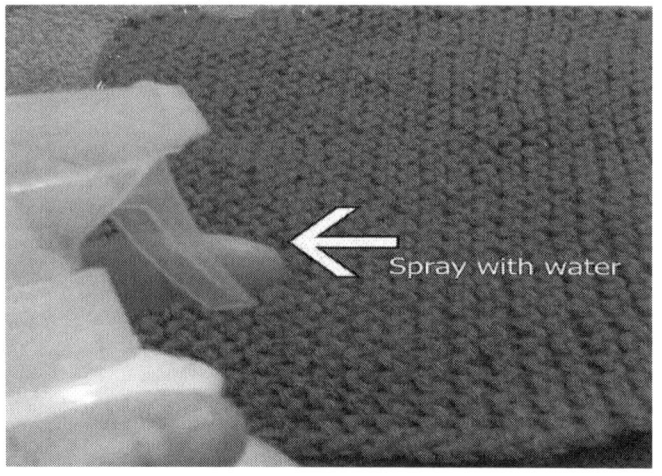

Illustration 114: Spray

3. Leave the project sit without being disturbed until it is dry.

Households with pets may want to set a damp towel over the project so pet hair does not collect on it. Just dampen the towel with the spray bottle. It is advised to always use a color-fast towel with any blocking method so as not to transfer the dye from the towel to the project.

Cotton and wool yarn block best as follows:

Steam Blocking

4. Preheat the iron to the wool setting

Illustration 115: Set Temperature on Iron

5. Lay the project on the padded board wrong side up. Stretch and pin as normal, but do not use pins with plastic tops that can melt.

Illustration 116: Prepare Project

6. Cover the project with a damp cloth or thin towel that will cover the entire project.

Illustration 117: Cover

7. Place the iron slightly over the top of the towel covering the project and steam until it is pressed.

Illustration 118: Steam

8. Let the project sit where it is until it is completely dry.

NEVER let the full weight of the iron sit on the project, in fact, never let the iron come in contact with the towel. If the iron has a steam jet feature that pulses a stream of steam by pushing a button, use it over the entire project. Certainly, NEVER let the iron touch the yarn of the project as some yarns will melt and cause damage to the project. Always steam the wrong side because some yarns become glossy and unnatural when heat comes in contact with them. This way the front will stay pristine.

Pieces that have a ribbing pattern that allows the project to stretch (see the Stitch Patterns section) should never be blocked as it will inhibit the stretch of the pattern.

Chapter 15: Care

In order to produce a great project, tare a few things that the knitter needs to do:

1. Always wash and dry hands and make sure they are clean before starting to knit. Nothing is worse that transferring dirt and grime to a project.

Illustration 119: Wash

2. Always save the label that comes with the yarn as there is a multitude of good information on it. Washing instructions are always included on the label and if they are not, do not purchase the skein. This is a very important piece of information. Also, on the label is the yarn weight and ply. This information might be needed if the project is to be made again. The lot number appears on the label too. This is important if the same color is desired. The lot number is a combination of numbers that tells what dye lot the yarn came from. You may

have two skeins of midnight blue yarn, but if one is from lot 40588 and the other is from 40601, they can be slightly different.

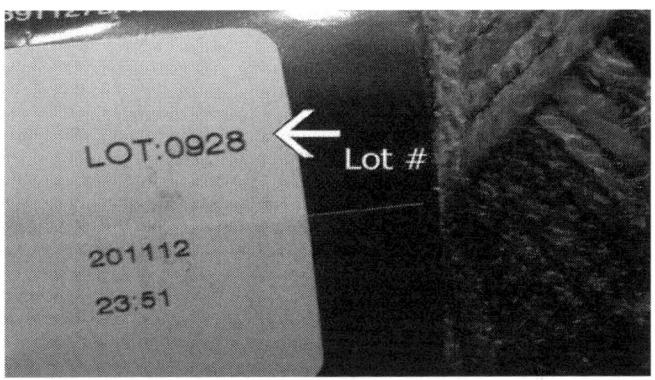

Illustration 120: Lot Number

3. Always follow washing instructions on the label. If the label says to hand wash and lay flat to dry, do not throw it in the washing machine and drier. You may end up with a sweater that will only fit a pixie because it will shrink drastically.

Illustration 121: Dry Flat

4. Work in a well-lit area. This allows for less mistakes because they are seen better in stronger light. Note that it is very hard to see dark colored yarns in dimly lit areas.
5. Never try to break the yarn instead of cutting it when a section or the project is complete. The yarn is made of several plies all twisted together. If it is broken, some of the plies may get out of shape and pull that causes the project to go out of kilter. Always use scissors or clippers to cut the yarn free from the skein.

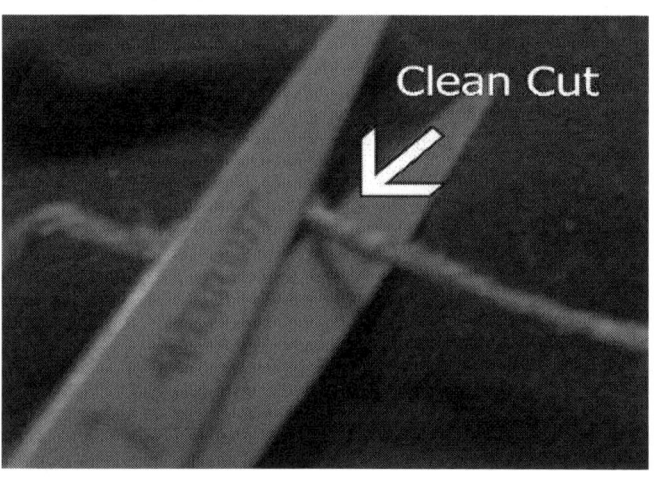

Illustration 122: Cut

6. Keep unused knitting needles in a safe place. It is best to bind the two needles together with a rubber band, so that one will not be lost. Put them in a jar, a vase or some other type of holder.

Illustration 123: Needle Storage

7. Keep leftover and saved yarn in a dry area so that it will not become moldy. Nothing is worse that smelling moldy yarn while knitting.

Illustration 124: Yarn Storage

8. After blocking a project, fold it and lay it flat. Putting a sweater on a hanger causes it to stretch out of shape and the hanger will put little bumps in the shoulders.

Illustration 125: Fold Flat

Chapter 16: Stitch Patterns

Different combinations of knit, purl, increase and decrease stitches produce distinct patterns with in the body of the project. Many of the combinations, or patterns, are used so often they have their own names. Some patterns for projects will merely say to do the stockinette stitch for 5 inches. Some will tell you to do a rib stitch using 2 knit and 2 purl stitches for 10 inches and expect you to know what to do.

The following stitches are basic stitches that every knitter should know how to do.

The Knit Stitch or Garter Stitch

The knit or garter stitch is the simplest stitch pattern of all. Make a garter stitch by knitting every row. Either go back to the 20-stitch sampler or start a new one. Knit 10 rows.

The knit or garter stitch produces a ridged appearance with edges that stay relatively flat.

Illustration 126: Garter or Knit Stitch

The Stockinette Stitch

The stockinette stitch is also very easy to do. To make this stitch, knit one row and purl the next. On the sampler do 10 rows of the stockinette stitch as follows:

- Row 1 – Knit all stitches across
- Row 2 – Purl all stitches across
- Row 3-10 – Repeat row 1 and 2 until 10 rows are completed.

This stitch produces a neat and smooth surface. The edges do tend to roll making it perfect for rolled cuffs.

Illustration 127: Stockinette Stitch

The Moss or Seed Stitch

The moss or seed stitch employs the use of knit and purl as follows:

- Row 1 – Knit all stitches across
- Row 2 – Purl all stitches across

Looks just like the stockinette stitch so far, but that is where things change up a bit.

- Row 3 – Purl all stitches across (the stockinette stitch would be knitted on this row)
- Row 4 – Knit all stitches across

The moss or seed stitch has two rows the same, whereas the stockinette stitch keeps alternating back and forth between knit and purl.

After completing 4 rows on the sampler, repeat the pattern two more times so that there is a total of 16 rows of moss or seed stitch on the sampler.

The reason the stitch is called the moss stitch is because the pattern resembles bumpy moss growing up a tree. It is uneven, yet beautiful. It also is reminiscent of seeds scattered on the ground, giving it the other name of seed stitch.

Illustration 128: Moss or Seed Stitch

Ribbing Stitch

The ribbing stitch allows the project to stretch and snap back into shape. The stitch is perfect for the edge of a hat that stretches to fit the head. It stays put and won't fall off. The stitch also works well on the cuff of gloves, mittens or sleeves.

To make a simple ribbing stitch on the sampler do the following:

- Knit 2 stitches
- Pull the skein tail to the front of the piece between the two needles
- Purl 2 stitches
- Pull the skein tail to the back of the piece between the two needles
- Knit 2 stitches
- Pull the skein tail to the front of the piece between the two needles
- Purl 2 stitches
- Keep going all the way across the sampler between the two needles

The important part of this pattern is to keep moving the skein tail back and forth when changing from knit to purl and back again.

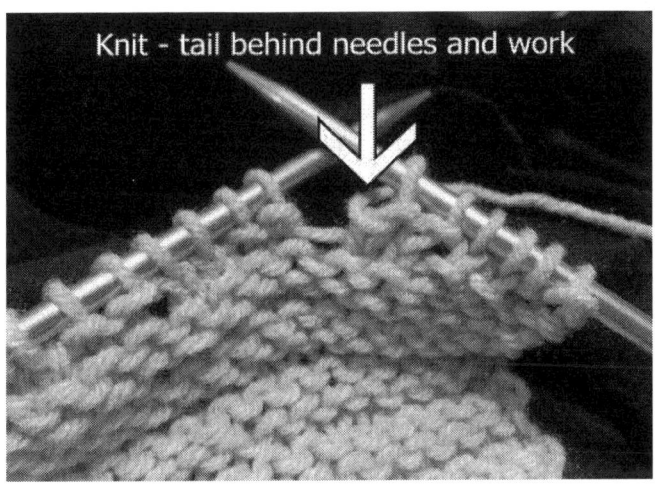

Illustration 129: Tail Position for Knit

Illustration 130: Tail Position for Purl

Complete the entire row. With 20 stitches, the row will end with 2 purl stitches. Turn the piece to start the 2nd row and start by Purling as indicated below:

- Purl 2 stitches
- Pull the skein tail to the back of the piece between the two needles
- Knit 2 stitches
- Pull the skein tail to the front of the piece between the two needles
- Purl 2 stitches
- Pull the skein tail to the back of the piece between the two needles
- Knit 2 stitches
- Complete the whole row.

Notice that if the last two stitches on the row are purl, the first two stitches in the next row are also purl. If there were 22 stitches on the sampler the last two stitches would have been knit stitches and when turned the first two would have been knit stitches. This manipulation of the stitches causes a vertical ridge in the project that is very stretchy and supple.

After a few rows in the sampler, a pattern emerges that allows the knitter to see which stitch to do when. The stitch above a knit stitch is smooth and looks like a "V".

Illustration 131: "V" of the Knit Stitch

The stitch above a purl stitch has a little bump and is not smooth at all.

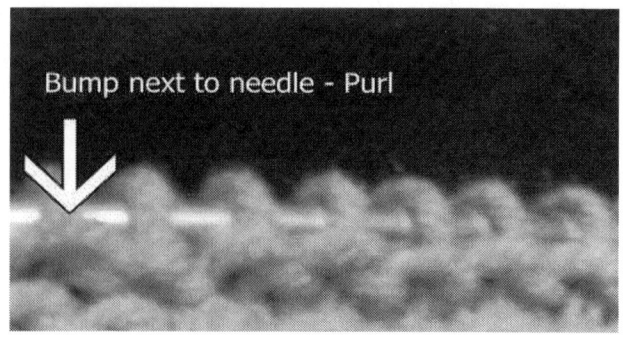

Illustration 132: Bump of Purl Stitch

Not moving the skein tail back and forth correctly causes extra stitches to appear seemingly out of nowhere and the piece begins to take on the shape of a triangle rather than the preferred rectangle.

On the sampler do 10 rows of the ribbing stitch. Complete 4 rows of the stockinette stitch after.

Ribbing is not always done with 2 knit and 2 purl stitches. A pattern might ask for 1 knit and 1 purl all along the row or opt for a wide ribbing with 5 knit stitches and 5 purl stitches. The pattern will dictate the number of each stitch within the row.

Illustration 133: Ribbing Stitch

Basket or Block Stitch

This unique stitch looks similar to a basket weave or little squares where the stitch goes up and down in one and side to side in the next. It resembles a patchwork quilt.

The total number of stitches on a needle must be divisible by 10 to do this particular pattern stitch. The sampler with 20 stitches is a perfect project as 20 divided by 10 is an even 2. From now on instructions will be written just as they would be in a pattern. Therefore, k means knit and p means purl. Watch for the symbol "*". The asterisk, or star, is an indication to go back to whatever was there after the asterisk and repeat either until the end or until the next asterisk. It isn't as hard as it sounds. See the explanation below.

Basket or Block stitch pattern for 20 stitches:

- Row 1 - *K5, p5. Repeat from * across the row, ending with p 5.

This means: Knit 5 stitches

Purl 5 stitches

Repeat the 5 knit stitches and the 5 purl stitches until the end of the row.

- Row 2 – 5 – Repeat Row 1 four more times
- Row 6 - * Purl 5, k5. Repeat from * across the row, ending with k5

This means: Purl 5 stitches

Knit 5 stitches

Repeat the 5 purl stitches and the 5 knit stitches until the end of the row.

- Row 7 – 10 – Repeat row 6 four more times

Repeat row 1 to row 10 two more times on the sampler

Illustration 134: Block or Basket Stitch

This stitch looks like a little quilt, bunch of blocks, or basket weave.

Thousands of different stitches exist including diamond shaped stitches, chevron stitches, zig zag stitches, lacey stitch and more. If a pattern uses a particular stitch, it will usually give the directors for that stitch before it starts the pattern. Within the pattern, it will state to do the chevron stitch for 4 inches.

It is a good idea to practice a new stitch before doing the pattern. Just cast on the amount of stitches required in the pattern for the stitch, and do several rows of the pattern. Once the pattern is achieved, just rip it out and start on the first step of the pattern.

Chapter 17: How to Join Seams

Seaming a knitted garment is very similar to putting seams in a cloth garment. Only stitch together seams after the pieces of the project are blocked. Some projects, such as hats, only require one seam. The piece is rolled around and stitched up one side or up the back. When making a sweater, many pieces may be involved. The front of the sweater may be in two pieces including the right and left front. The back is another piece and each sleeve is yet more pieces.

Always try to leave a long tail on each piece as it is finished. Use this tail to seam the pieces together. This eliminates the need for another piece of yarn that might come unraveled.

<u>Backstitch Seam</u>

The reason this stitch is called the backstitch seam is because the stitch moves backwards, or left to right, along the seam of the project.

Place project pieces together with right sides facing each other on the inside and wrong side facing outward. When stitching arm warmers that only have one seam, hold them so that the piece is inside-out.

Illustration 135: Right Sides Together

It is very important to match up the pieces so that one side is not longer than the other. In the case of the arm warmers, both ends should match up.

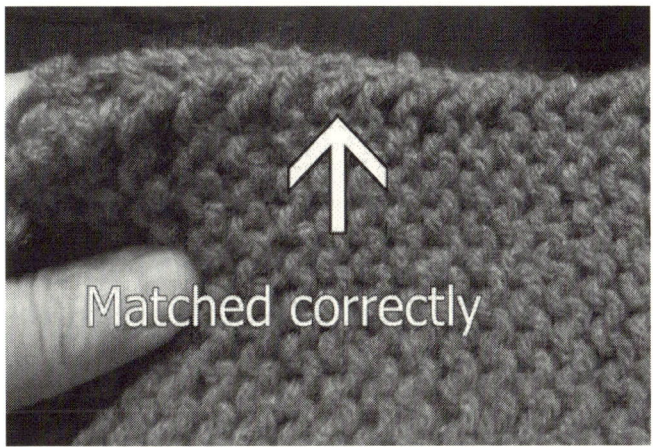

Illustration 136: Correct

Illustration 137: Incorrect

1. Thread the tail through a blunt, large-eye yarn needle.

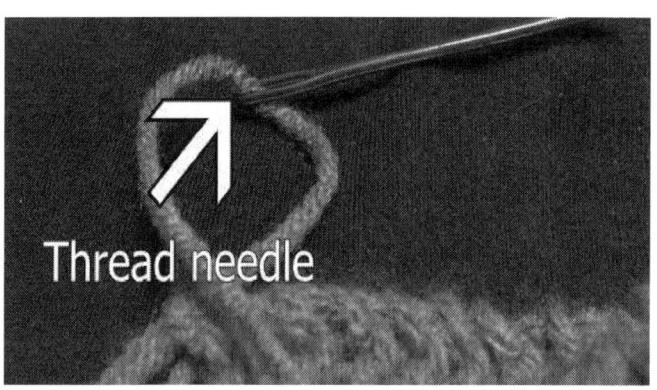

Illustration 138: Thread

2. Hold the piece with the tail attached edge to the left.

Illustration 139: Backstitch Position

3. Bring the needle away from the edge about ¼ inch away from the side edge and close to the horizontal edge. Insert the point of the needle and go to the left in a straight line.

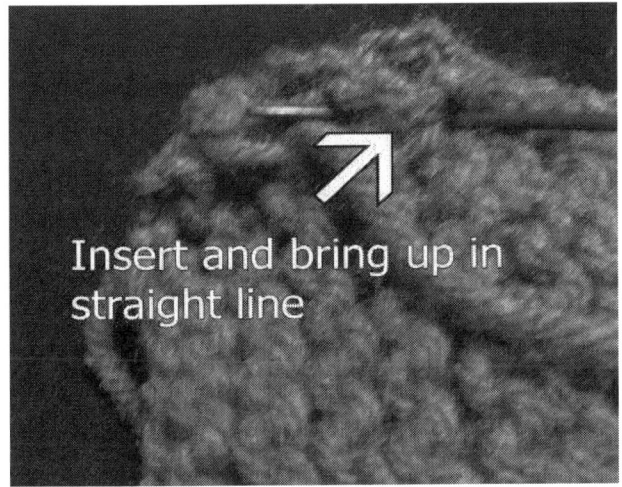

Illustration 140: Insert

4. Make sure the needle goes through both pieces and bring it back up to the top.

Illustration 141: Backstitch Form

5. Pull the tail to tighten the stitch, but not so much as to pucker the seam.

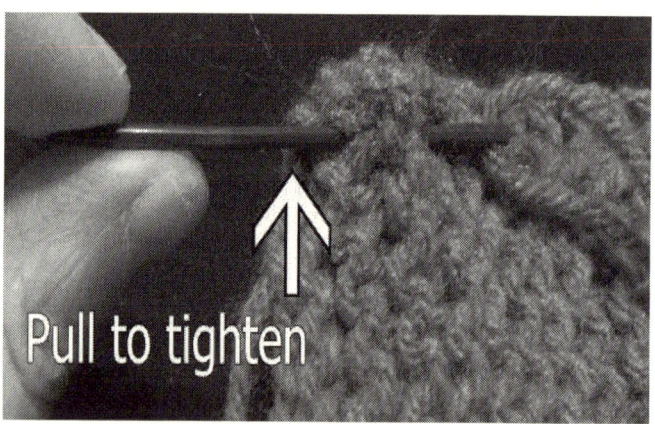

Illustration 142: Tighten

6. Insert the point of the needle just a little further to the right of the first stitch.

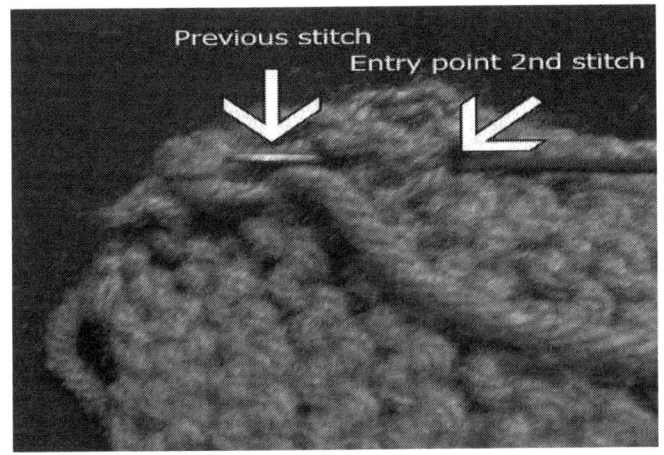

Illustration 143: Second Stitch

7. Poke all the way through and to the left bringing it back up to the top just a little further than where the tail emerges in a straight line.

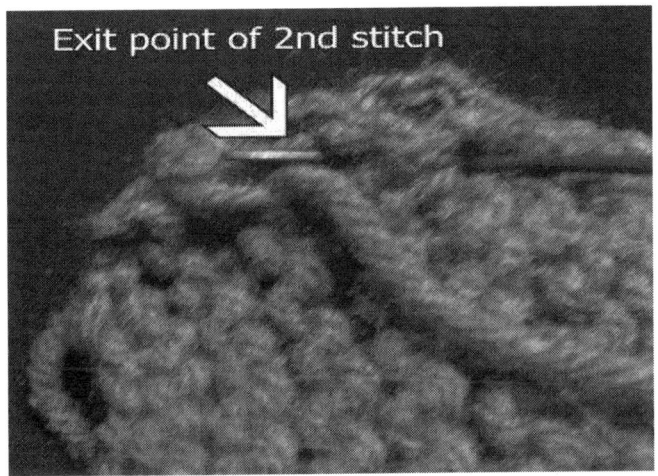

Illustration 144: Straight Line

8. Pull and keep moving toward the right until the end is reached. Make a knot.

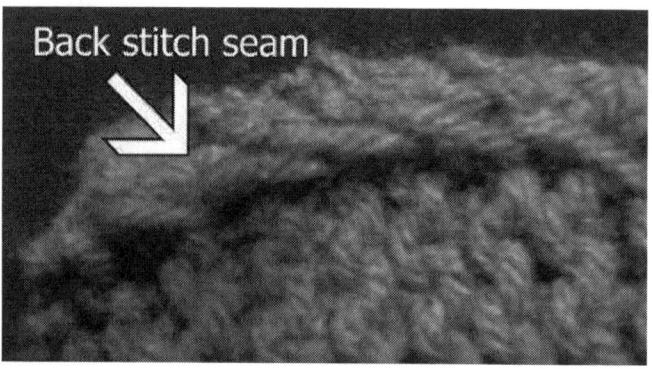

Illustration 145: Seam

9. Cut tail a few inches long and weave into the project.

Whip Stitch

In the whip stitch the stitch is whipped around the seam again and again.

Prepare pieces right sides together and wrong sides out.

1. Thread the needle and bring it through both pieces from back to front at the edge of the seam.

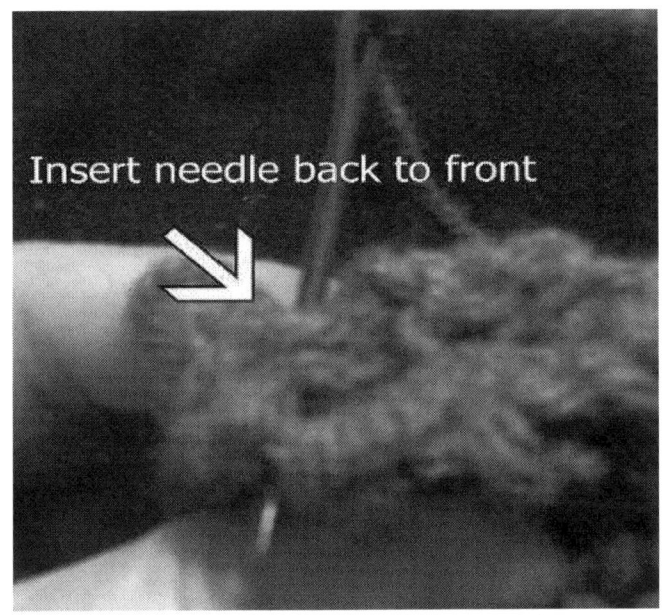

Illustration 146: Back to Front Whip Stitch

2. Bring the needle up and over the seam.

Illustration 147: Whip Tail Over

3. Insert needle in the back near the seam and bring it through all pieces to the front working to the right.

Illustration 148: Insert and Pull

4. Again, bring the needle up and over the seam to the right, insert the needle from back to front and pull. Do not pull too tight or the seam will pucker.

Illustration 149: Whip and Pull

5. Continue to the end of the piece. Knot the yarn and cut tail and weave it in.

This method causes the seams to be a little bit bulky, but they hold very well.

Invisible Seam

Complete this method by joining two pieces on the right side along the edges. It works well for side seams and is virtually invisible. It is very important to match each side up line by line perfectly. If this not lined up correctly, the front of a sweater might be several inches longer than it is in the back.

1. Place pieces right side up on a flat surface.

Illustration 150: Prepare Project

2. Insert the threaded needle through the end stich on the garment piece on the right.

Illustration 151: Insert

3. Bring the needle through the end stitch on the left-hand piece from back to front.

Illustration 152: Stitch Through Back

4. Move the needle through the back of the second stich on the right-hand piece and bring it to the front.

Illustration 153: Stitch Through Front

5. Continue going up one stitch matching stitch for stich from right to left until the seam is completed. Pull after each stitch, but not so

much as to pucker the seam. Then knot, cut and weave.

Chapter 18: Scarf Pattern

A scarf is the best pattern to use in order to learn how to knit. It is very repetitious and there are not curves or turns in the patterns. There are also no seams, making it much simpler than some other patterns like sweaters. A scarf is something that the beginner can do successfully without much help.

This scarf is mostly made up of the stockinette stitch, but because the stockinette stitch tends to roll, a border of garter stitches is done so it stays relatively flat.

The scarf is lovely made of one color, or instead, try two different colors of yarn to make stripes. Just count 10 to 20 rows between each color change.

This pattern makes a moderately wide scarf. A thinner scarf would require fewer cast on stitches and a wider scarf that is easily folded longwise for extra warmth needs more stitches. Make it as long as desired. Use fewer rows for a scarf that just crosses in the front and use more rows for a scarf that wraps around the neck a few times.

The pattern does use common abbreviations, but because beginners don't always remember all the abbreviations, easy to understand instructions are included in parenthesis. One size fits all for this pattern.

Scarf Pattern

Illustration 154: Easy Scarf

You will need:

Size 8 knitting needles (US)

1 Skein 4-ply yarn or 2 skeins if making stripes

Scissors

Hardback book

Crochet hook (size F to I) (it doesn't matter what size, just don't try to use a tiny hook)

Pattern:

CO 30 sts (Cast on 30 stitches)

Row 1 – 6: K across row (knit across row)

Row 7: K 5, p 30, k 5 (knit 5 stitches, purl 30 stitches, knit 5 stitches)

Row 8: K across row

Repeat rows 7 and 8 until scarf is the desired length.

Last 5 Rows: K across rows, CO on last row (knit across the last 5 rows and cast off)

Weave tail into the scarf and add fringe.

Fringe is easy to add and lends a finished, decorative look to the scarf. If preferred, leave the fringe off. A thin fringe uses 2 to 3 strands of yarn for each piece of fringe. A thicker fringe requires 5 to 6 strands.

To add fringe:

1. Wrap yarn around a hardback book landscape-wise. Wrap 25 to 50 times.

Illustration 155: Wrap Yarn

2. Cut off the skein tail near the binding of the book

Illustration 156: Cut Tail

3. Cut yarn across the indentation of the pages of the book in landscape fashion.

Illustration 157: Cut to Make Fringe

4. Gather two to three pieces of yarn for a thin fringe and five to six pieces for a thick fringe. Fold them in half.

Illustration 158: Gather

5. Insert the crochet hook from back to front in the end edge stitch of the scarf. Fringe can be added from left to right or right to left. Do whatever seems comfortable to you.

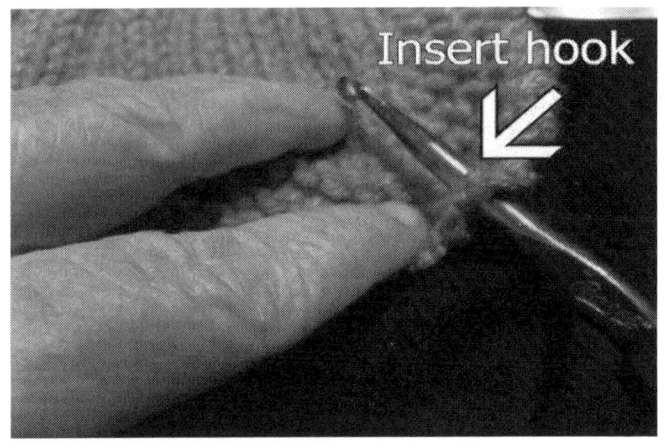

Illustration 159: Insert Hook

6. Hook the middle of the fringe pieces.

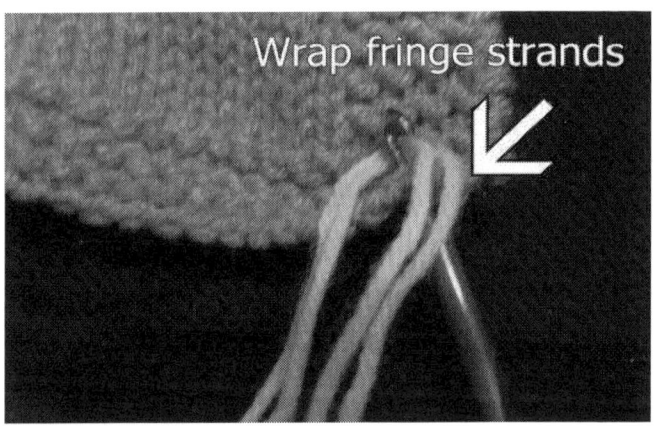

Illustration 160: Hook Middle

7. Pull the fringe pieces partially through to the back making a loop.

Illustration 161: Pull

8. Catch the ends of the fringe tails and pull through the loop.

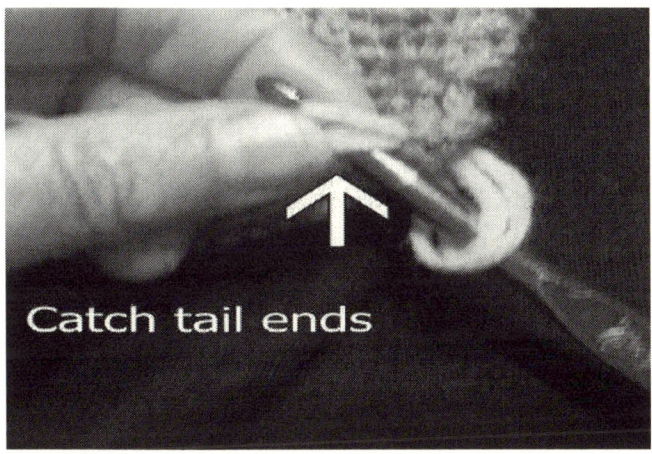

Illustration 162: Pull Ends Through Loop

9. Pull the ends through the loop creating a knot.

Illustration 163: Beginning Knot

10. Pull all the way through and pull tight.

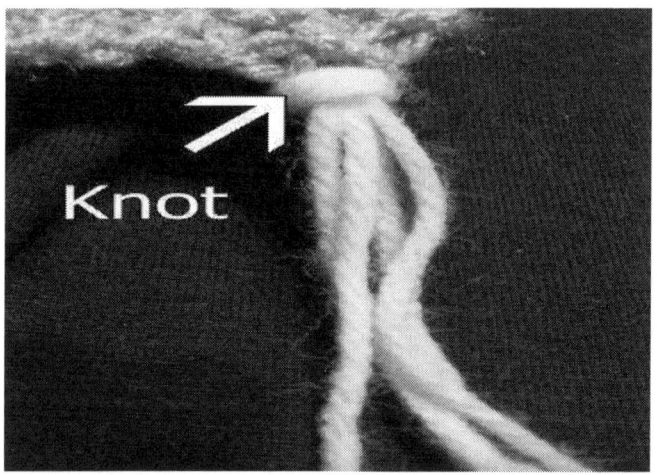

Illustration 164: Knot

11. Continue to add fringe down the entire edge of the scarf and do the other short side of the scarf. Always make sure to insert the hook from back to front or you will have some knots on

one side of the scarf and some on the other. This doesn't make for a uniform appearance.

Illustration 165: Add More Fringe

12. Lay scarf on a flat surface and trim the fringe to make it all even.

Illustration 166: Trim

Chapter 19: Arm Warmer Pattern

Illustration 167: Arm Warmer

This arm warmer pattern uses both the rib stitch with 2 knit stitches and 2 purl stitches and the stockinette stitch. It also needs to have a seam put in. Use either the back stitch or whip stitch, explained in the Seam chapter, to sew the arm warmer together. Of course, make two arm warmers. This pattern has numbers in parenthesis to indicate different sizes. The number outside the parenthesis is for a small, the first one inside the parenthesis is for medium, the next large and the last extra-large. Usually a small is for a 6-inch wrist, medium for a 7-inch wrist, large for 7 1/2-inch wrist and extra-large at an 8-inch wrist.

Do some variations on this pattern just like in the scarf pattern. Do the ribbing in one color and the rest in another or make it striped like the scarf.

You will need:

Size US 5 needles

1 skein 4-ply yarn

Straight pins

1 blunt, yarn needle

Gauge: 22 st = 4"; 32 rows = 4". This means that 22 stitches should measure 4 inches and 32 rows should also measure 4 inches. Do a swatch 22 stitches with 32 rows. Measure to make sure the stitch is accurate.

Arm Warmer Pattern

CO 34 (38, 42, 46) sts

- Row 1: K2, p2, to the last 2 stitches, k2 - This means knit 2 stitches, purl 2 stitches and keep alternating until 2 stitches are left on the needle. Knit those 2 stitches
- Row 2: P2, k2, to the last 2 stitches, p2 - This means purl 2 stitches, knit 2 stitches and keep alternating until 2 stitches are left on the needle. Purl those 2 stitches.
- Repeat row 1 and 2until piece measures 1 ½ (2, 2 ½, 3)", end with a wrong side row. This means keep doing row 1 and 2 until correct measurement is reached and end with a purl row.
- Work St st until piece measures 2 ¼ (3, 3 ½, 4 ¼)" from beginning, end after a wrong side row. - This means keep doing the stockinette stitch until correct measurement is reached and end with a purl row.

- Inc 1 st every 8th row at the beg and end. Do this 8 (8, 8, 10) times to make 50 (54, 58, 66) total sts. – This means increase 1 stitch at the beginning and end of every 8th row. Start at the current row and increase one stitch on stitch 1 and one stitch on the last stitch. Do this at the 8th, 16th, 24th, 32nd, 40th, 48th, 56th row.
- Work until piece measures 13 (13 ½, 14, 15)" from beginning to end, ending with a wrong side row. - If the piece doesn't quite measure the correct amount of inches by the time the 50 to 66 stitches are complete, keep doing the stockinette stitch without adding more stitches until it does.
- Change the st to k2, p2 rib stitch for 1 ½ (2, 2 ½, 3)", end with a wrong side row
- BO – This means bind off.

Finishing:

Using a blunt yarn needle, use the cut tail to sew the side seam from top (wide end) to leaving a 1" area unsewn about 1" from the cast on edge for a thumbhole. Weave in all ends.

Chapter 20: Tips and Tricks

The following are tips and tricks that seasoned knitters use to make their work more beautiful and make knitting easier.

Needles

Sometimes needles get a bit dull and the stitches just do not flow on and off as easily as they should. Metal and plastic needles are easy to fix. Just run the needle, tip first, through your hair being careful not to poke your scalp too hard. The oils from the scalp lubricate the needles and the stitches will no longer stick.

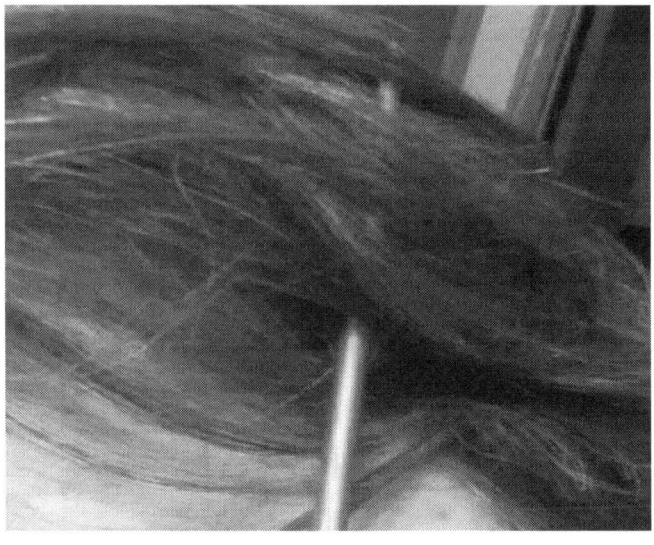

Illustration 168: Lubricate Needles - Hair

Rub the plastic or metal needles with a square of wax paper and get the same benefit without the human factor.

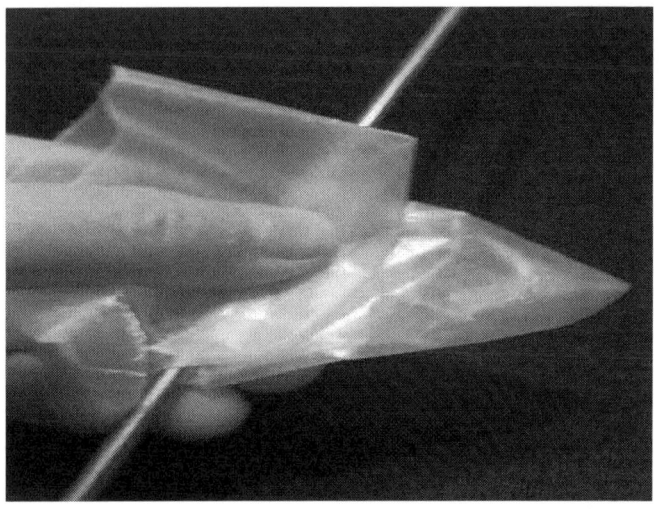

Illustration 169: Lubricating Needles - Wax Paper

Bamboo needles tend to get a little rough after use. The wood lightly splinters causing the yarn to stick and pull. The wax paper trick works on bamboo and rubbing a drier sheet usually will help. If the rough spot is too rough take an Emery board or fingernail file to the area and sand it down. Wipe off the rough patch and when you start knitting again, the stitches should move freely.

Storage

Proper storage of all knitting paraphernalia and yarn is very important. Yarn can become moldy if it gets wet and then it is no longer usable. Bending or breaking knitting needles renders them useless as well.

Needles

Store needles upright if at all possible. Place them in a knitting needle holder, a tall empty can, oatmeal box or in a vase.

Illustration 170: Needle Holder

If you must put them in a drawer, do not store things on top of them. Heavy objects can cause the needles to curve and for best knitting results, they need to be straight.

Wrap needle pairs with a rubber band to keep them together. This is especially important with double pointed needles as they rarely have the size imprinted on them. Just make a label, punch a hole in it and put the rubber band through before securing the needles.

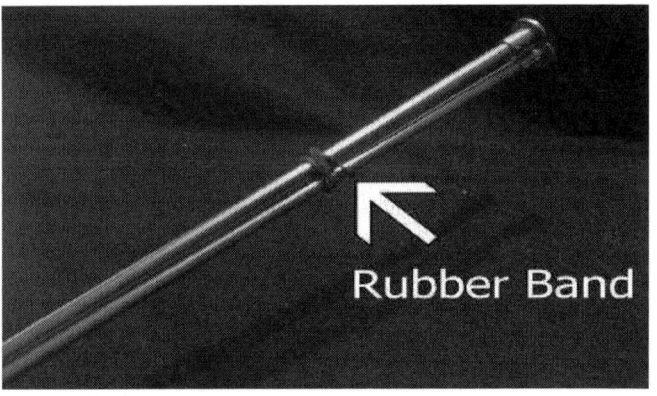

Illustration 171: Secure Needles with Rubber Bands

Patterns

Patterns come from a variety of sources. Books have knitting patterns in them as do magazines. Get patterns from the computer and download them onto white paper. Pick up small size pamphlets at stores that sell yarn provided by the companies that produce the yarn. Patterns come in all sizes and shapes and storage can sometimes be a problem. It is important to store them neatly so that they are able to be used again and again.

Purchase a three-ring binder and large and small size plastic, see-through page protectors. Put the protectors in the book and store pattern booklets in the protectors. Get several of the pamphlets and put them in another protector and always put the printed instructions in a plastic protector. Keep the pattern inside the protector while using it and it will stay clean and fresh. This ensures patterns will stay clean and flat to be used for years to come.

Illustration 172: Pattern Binder

For those that amass large quantities of patterns, organize them into several binders. Keep baby clothes in one, sweaters in another, hats in another binder and so on.

Tails

Beginner knitters always get the tails mixed up. It must be a rite of passage or something. There is the Cast On tail used ONLY to cast on and never used again until it is time to seam a piece together. Then there is the Skein tail attached to the skein. Use this tail while knitting. To get that cast on tail out of the way roll it up into a little bundle and then wrap a twisty tie from a bread wrapper around it. Make sure it stays in that little bundle and you will never mistake it for the tail you actually need to use.

Illustration 173: Tie Cast-On Tail

Discerning Right from Wrong Side

After knitting several projects it will be easy to tell which side is the right side and which is not. Until that is learned, use some of these nifty methods to tell which side is which at a glance.

- The cast on tail, the one held in the twisty tie, is always oat the bottom left of the right side of the piece.

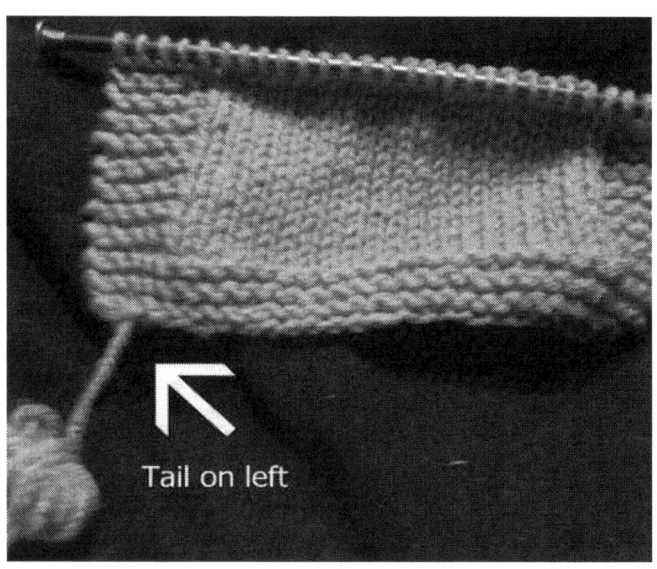

Illustration 174: Tail Position Method

- Purchase two pairs of the same size knitting needle in two different colors. Use one color for the right side and the other for the left. EXAMPLE: Cast on stitches to a red needle and knit the first row with a green needle. The green needle will always be the right side and the red will be the wrong side. Be careful to always use two metal needles or two plastic ones and never mix the two. It might make for uneven knitting. Also be aware some manufacturers may say the needles are both size 8, but there might be a slight difference. Try to get the different colored needles from the same manufacturer.

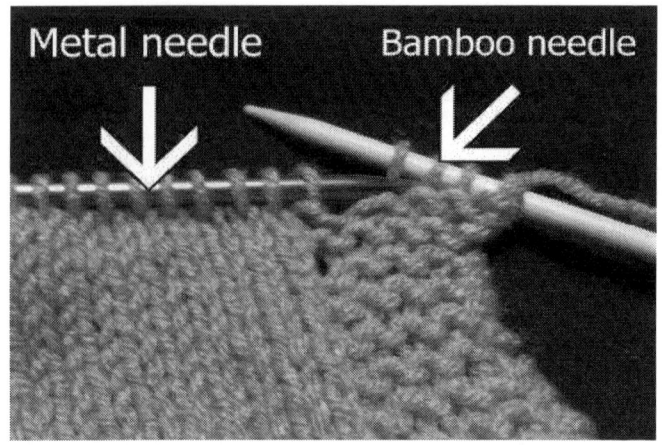

Illustration 175: Colored Needle Method

- Remember those rubber bands used to keep needles together while in storage? Wrap them around one of the needles near the top stopper. The needle with the rubber band attached will be the right side and the one without will be the wrong side. When knitting is finished the rubber bands will be right there and you won't have to search for them.

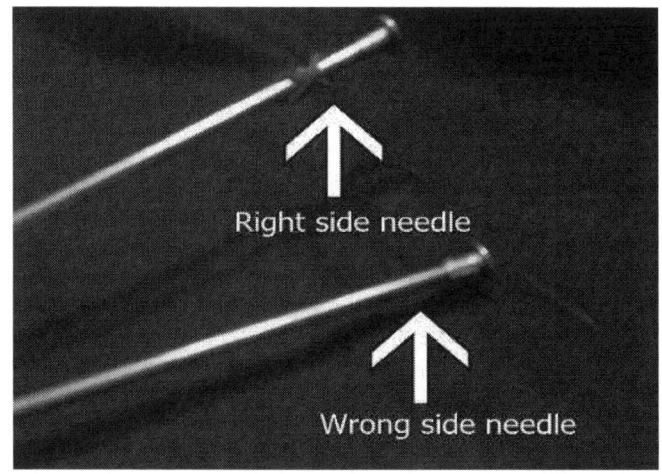

Illustration 176: Rubber Band Method

Counting Rows

Counting rows is difficult in a complex pattern especially when there are distractions like cats, dogs, kids and significant others around. A row counter helps, but sometimes it is possible to miss flipping the number to the next digit. The following are a few ways to keep track of rows:

- Keep a little notebook or index card and pencil nearby as you knit. When a row is completed, mark the row number down.

Illustration 177: Notebook/Index Card Method

- Put a stitch marker at the beginning of each row. It is easier to count stitch markers that strain the eyes to find the rows. Use different colors for each row or just count every 5 rows or so. This tends to take a lot of stitch markers, but it will help to count rows.

Illustration 178: Stitch Marker Method

- Use a regular piece of 8 ½ x 11 inch paper to count rows. Every time a row is completed, fold the paper like a fan, one section per row. EXAMPLE: Row one is finished so the paper is held landscape and one fold from top to bottom is made at the end of the paper.

Illustration 179: One Row - One Fold

When the next row is completed another fold of the fan is made.

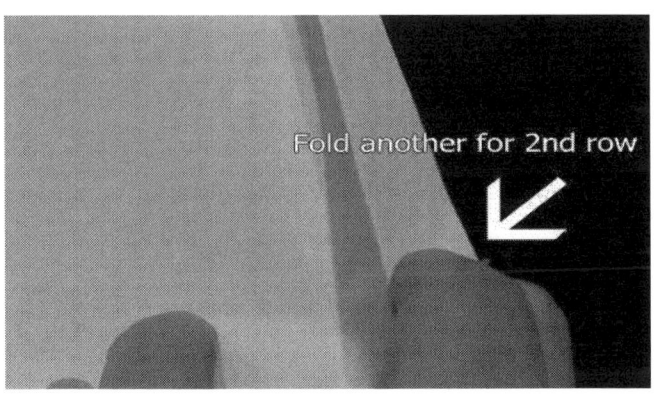

Illustration 180: Two Rows - Two Folds

Use a paper clip to keep the fan stable. Count each fold to see how many rows have been done.

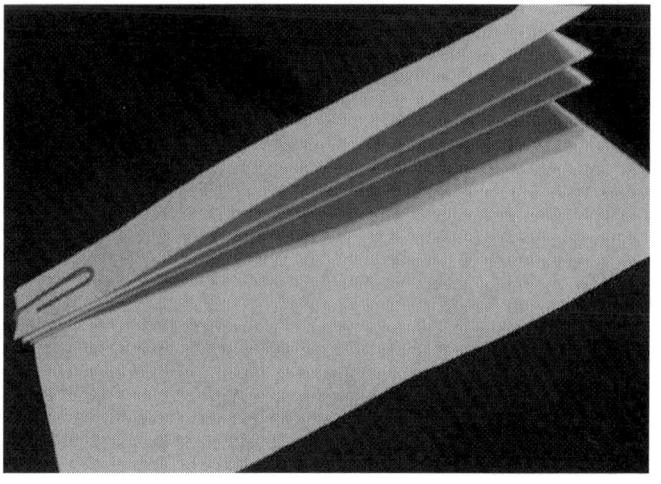

Illustration 181: Secure with Paper Clip

Find a comfortable well-lit place to knit. Have everything you need right there and ready to go. Keep yarn in a basket along with stitch markers, extra needles, scissors and other necessary accessories. It is a proven fact that yarn releases from the skein much better when it is on the floor and drawn upwards. Keep skeins or balls in a plastic a grocery bag with the yarn coming out one of the handles tied in to keep yarn from rolling all over the room. It keeps the yarn clean and prevents pets and children from getting into it. Cats particularly love yarn and if they ingest it, it can wrap around their intestines and cause a great deal of harm. Some yarn even comes in a bag that just releases the tail.

Illustration 182: Bagged Skein

Illustration 183: Grocery Bag Method

Use a music stand set near the knitting chair to hold the pattern. It will always be in site and holds the pattern up so that it is easy to see. Music stands come very cheap and are very easy to find.

Illustration 184: Music Stand

Edges

Keeping edges neat and tight is important. A messy edge makes for a messy, irregular product. Keeping edges straight is important when a seam is in the edge's future. It is very hard to match up a sloppy edge and easy to match a neat one. No one likes a sleeve where the one edge is 3 inches longer than the other side. Here are a few methods that will keep edges on the straight and narrow:

- Knit into the back of the stitch on the last stitch on the needle. Then purl into the first stitch of every row. This tightens up those edges.

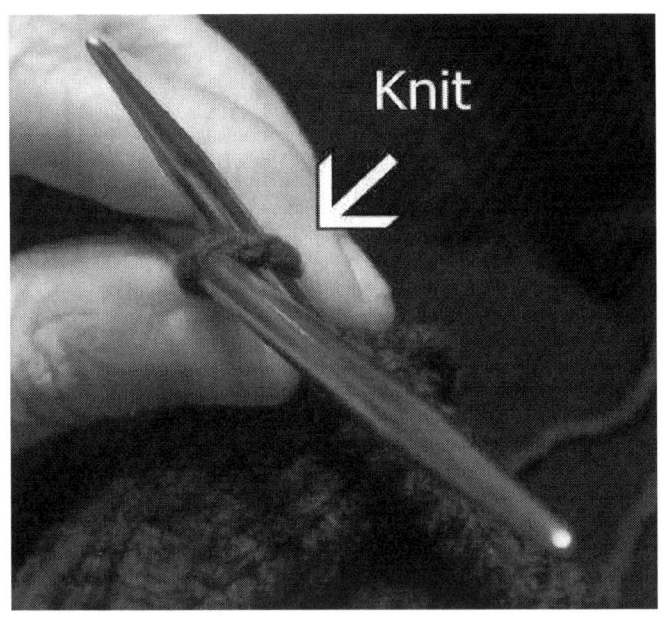

Illustration 185: Knit in Back

- Do not knit or purl the first stitch in every row. Instead, just slip it over to the carrier needle. If it is a knit stitch, slip over knitwise. If it is a purl stitch, slip over purlwise. Don't worry that it will cause problems in the pattern because the stitch compensates in the next row.

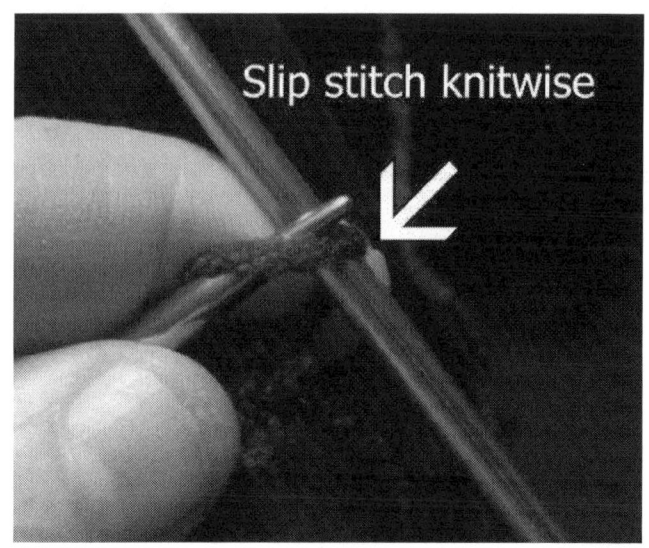

Illustration 186: Slip Knitwise

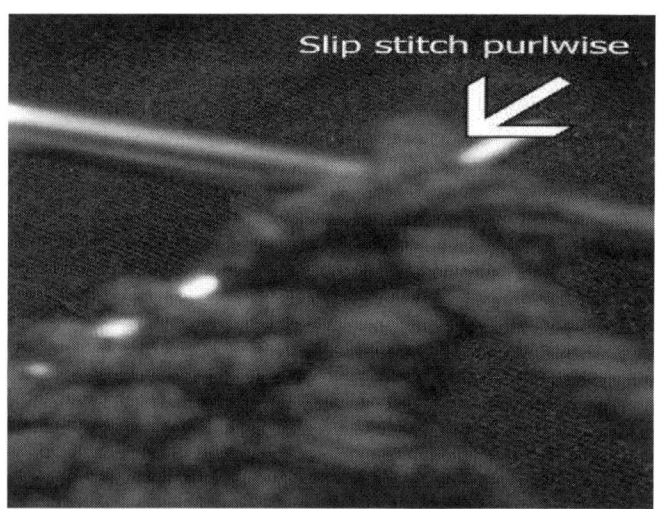

Illustration 187: Slip Purlwise

Stitch Markers

Stitch markers are necessary in some patterns and the little plastic rings can cost a lot of money. Make your own stitch markers out of things that are lying around the house.

- Use twisty ties from bread wrappers instead of plastic markers. Just wrap them around the needle and tie so they are loose and have the ability to slip over to the next needle in the next row. Just secure them with a twist.

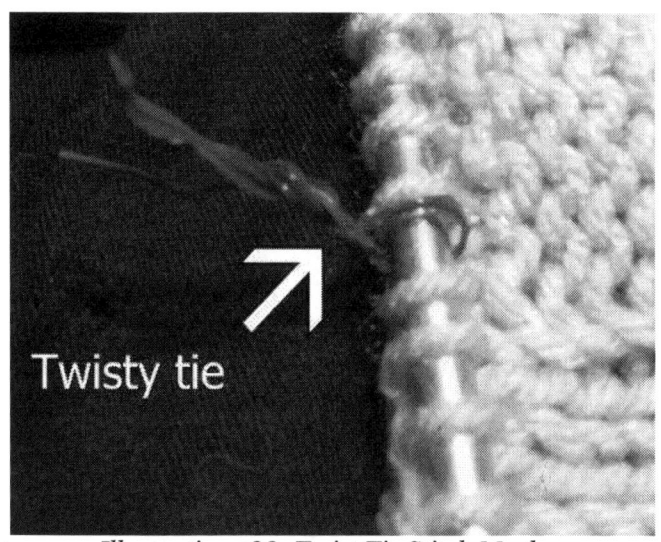

Illustration 188: Twist Tie Stitch Marker

- Use paper clips as stitch markers by inserting one end into the stitch and bringing it up to the bend in the clip. Use brightly colored, plastic coated paper clips in the small size. They are small enough to not tangle in the knitting and are color coded.

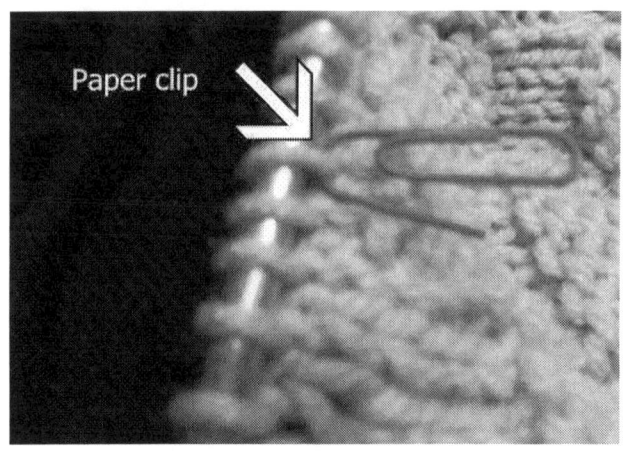

Illustration 189: Paper Clip Stitch Marker

- Bobby pins are another stitch marker alternative. Just insert one end into the stitch.
- Take plastic straws and cut into small rounds with scissors.

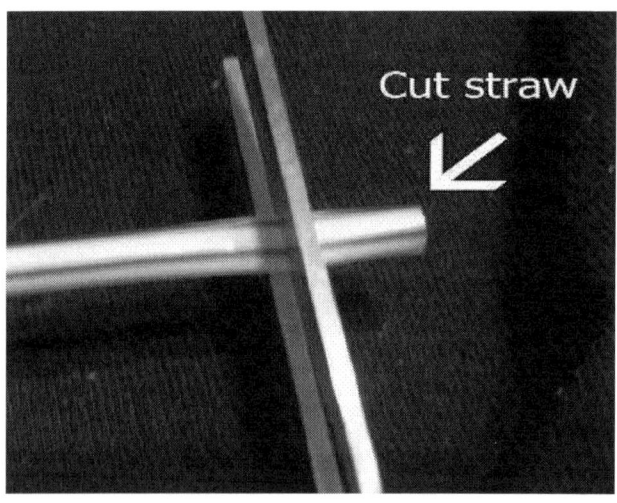

Illustration 190: Cut to Make Straw Stitch Marker

These fit over the needle and are easily slipped back and forth.

When using thinner needles, use paper reinforcement rings, the kind that stick over the holes in notebook paper to make them strong. Take two and stick them together, gummy sides facing each other so they stick together. Just slip them on the needle to mark the stitches.

Seaming

Using many straight pins to pin pieces of a garment together is a real pain. The needles do not like to stick into knitted fiber as they do in woven fabric and the tail gets stuck on them as the piece is being sewed together. Instead of using pins, use another straight knitting needle to secure the pieces together before seaming. Just push the point through the top and back up through the bottom. Now there is nothing to catch the tail and the pieces hold together very well.

Illustration 191: Hold Seams Together

Binding Off

Binding off too tight causes a pucker at the end of the garment. To avoid this problem, bind off with a needle one or two sizes larger than the original needle. It loosens up those stitches and makes them look neat and tidy. Just pick up the bigger needle on the row that is to be bound off.

Illustration 192: Bind Off Trick

The very last stitch that is done when binding off is often loose. To avoid a loose stitch, bind off the last two stitches together. It won't compromise the pattern and there will no long be one big looped stitch at the end.

Miscellaneous

- It is very confusing when patterns indicate several different sizes. They print the smallest size with three or four other sizes in parenthesis. EXAMPLE: knit 8 (9, 10, 11) or continue to do stockinette stich for 4 (4 ½, 5, 5 ½)". The original number is for small, the first one in the parenthesis is for medium, the next one is for large and the last for extra-large. To lessen confusion, copy the pattern and either highlight the numbers used for the size desired or use a marker and cross of the other size increments.

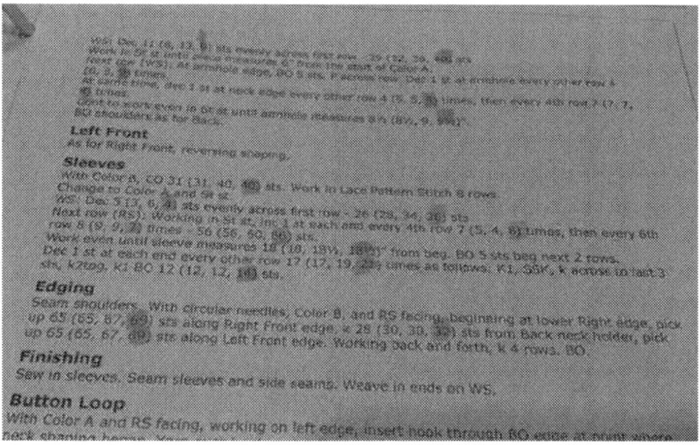

Illustration 193: Highlight Pattern

- Use cork or foam ear plugs as needle stoppers. Put them on the pointed ends of the needle when taking a rest from knitting and the stitches won't fall off. Winding a rubber band around the end of the needle will also hold the stitches on.

Illustration 194: Cork Stitch Stopper

- When a skein is almost used, employ this method to see if there is enough yarn left to complete the row. Stretch out the stitches on the needle as far as they will go, but not so far as they fall off. Stretch the remaining yarn out over the stretched out stitches and if it will go back and forth four times, there is enough yarn. If it doesn't, end at the closest row and join the new skein.

Illustration 195: Enough Yarn to Finish Row

Chapter 21: Conclusion

Knitting is not hard. Learning the stitches and abbreviations for patterns is half the battle. Before long, beginning knitters are creating scarves and baby blankets with fines. Soon they become competent at hats, mittens and knitted bags. Even those with just a little experience can craft a simple sweater, shawl or afghan in which to snuggle on cold night.

Knitting is proven to calm a person. This is because it takes some concentration and the repetitive movements of the hands relax the body and mind.

It won't be long before the beginning knitter starts to see where a pattern is easily altered to fit their own needs, and they start to create their own patterns.

Pretty soon they move on to more advanced projects like baby clothes, gloves and might even try to tackle a sock using three to four double pointed needles or circular needles.

Nothing is better than going to a baby shower with a hand knitted gift. Make a baby sweater, hat and baby blanket and the whole room will be thrilled to see the talent of the knitter. Make members of the family hats and scarves custom-made with their favorite colors. Knit a grocery bag that will never have to be thrown in the land fill or make a custom pillow for the living room sofa.

Illustration 196: Baby Sweater and Hat

Illustration 197: Scarf Using Textured Yarn

Yarn comes in such a variety of thicknesses, textures and colors that the possibilities are endless. It is gratifying to know that you can create so many useful and beautiful things with just a little string of fiber and two or more long needles.

Knitting Through the Ages

It used to be that when mentioning knitting, an old lady sitting in a rocker on the front porch was envisioned. Knitting was a past time for old women, but that is not the case anymore. Many people have taken up the needles and are learning to knit from grade school kids to teens to housewives, businessmen and construction workers.

Weaving, knitting's precursor, uses a frame in order to combine thread or yarn into material. Knitting does not use a frame. Two needles knot yarn or thread into a somewhat solid piece of material. The word knit comes from the English word "knot" that comes from a Dutch word "knutten", meaning knot. The origin of knitting is controversial. Some say it came from Spain, some from the Middle East and others think it came from Egypt. The person that invented knitting was certainly brilliant because they figured out how to use two sticks to weave yarn into a wearable piece of clothing.

One of the first known pieces of knitting comes from Egypt and dates to 1000 CE. It is a pair of white and indigo colored socks called the Coptic socks. The fiber used for the socks is cotton, not wool as expected. Wool did not make an appearance in knit form until many years later.

Many examples of ancient knit work are extremely complicated made of different colors of formed into geometric shapes. Therefore, knitting might be a little older than originally thought. These geometric shapes take some figuring and it would take a long time to perfect a pattern for such pieces.

Knitting became a popular during the Renaissance when stockings were made from the knit stitch. Portraits painted of the Virgin Mary during the mid-1300 showed her knitting, and in the 1500s the purl stitch, opposite to the knit stitch, was introduced. The Scots were well known for their Aran knits, which were made from lamb's wool that kept fishermen dry and warm. Whole families knitted, including the shepherds in the field, in order to supply the world with these beautiful knits. During this time not only women knitted, but also children and men. The profession of a knitter was revered and knitters made stockings, socks, jackets, sweaters, coats, pillows and other useful items.

The Industrial Revolution mechanized knitting producing more that cost less. The delight of knitting a family member a sweater was put by the wayside and ready-made knitwear became available. Resurgence came during the First World War when patterns, yarn and needles were issued so citizens could knit gloves and scarves for the Army and Navy to keep them warm in the winter. After the war different yarn colors and textures were developed and the fashion industry embraced knitwear. Toys, bags, curtains and more were being knitted in addition to clothing.

Knitting is considered a popular hobby today. People knit hand bags, scarves, gloves, skirts, baby clothing, blankets and other items. The variety of yarns is expansive and patterns abound in print and on the

Internet. The variety of stitches is astounding and anyone with a creative spark can think up a new and improved knitting pattern that will suit just about anyone.

About the Expert

Deborah C. Harding is a freelance writer living in North Eastern Ohio. She has been writing for over 20 years and has two published books including The Green Guide to Herb Gardening that details how to grow and use 10 easy herbs, and KidStuff that explains how to play with preschoolers in order to help them learn.

Deborah has a degree in Music Education from Youngstown State University and is an accomplished Musician. She has been a choir and worship leader at several churches, plays guitar and harp and sings in a professional choir.

Deborah learned to knit from her grandmother and mother when she was about six years old and is proficient in knitting and crochet teaching classes for 4-H kids.

HowExpert publishes quick 'how to' guides on all topics from A to Z by everyday experts. Visit HowExpert.com to learn more.

Recommended Resources

- HowExpert.com – Quick 'How To' Guides on All Topics from A to Z by Everyday Experts.
- HowExpert.com/free – Free HowExpert Email Newsletter.
- HowExpert.com/books – HowExpert Books
- HowExpert.com/courses – HowExpert Courses
- HowExpert.com/clothing – HowExpert Clothing
- HowExpert.com/membership – HowExpert Membership Site
- HowExpert.com/affiliates – HowExpert Affiliate Program
- HowExpert.com/writers – Write About Your #1 Passion/Knowledge/Expertise & Become a HowExpert Author.
- HowExpert.com/resources – Additional HowExpert Recommended Resources
- YouTube.com/HowExpert – Subscribe to HowExpert YouTube.
- Instagram.com/HowExpert – Follow HowExpert on Instagram.
- Facebook.com/HowExpert – Follow HowExpert on Facebook.

Made in United States
Orlando, FL
22 July 2025

63174185R00095